1998-612

J
523.8   GALLANT, ROY A.
Gal   Private lives of the stars

DATE DUE		
FEB 25 1999		

DO NOT PROCESS

Private Lives of the

STARS

ROY A. GALLANT

Private Lives of the

STARS

Macmillan Publishing Company
New York
Collier Macmillan Publishers
London

1998 — 712

Title page photograph courtesy of Palomar Observatory
Diagrams on pages 41, 55, 59, and 67 courtesy of Science Photo/Graphics, Inc.
Book design by Constance Ftera
Macmillan Publishing Company
866 Third Avenue, New York, NY 10022
Collier Macmillan Canada, Inc.
First Edition
Printed in the United States of America
10 9 8 7 6 5 4 3 2 1
The text of this book is set in 12 point Bembo.
The illustrations are black-and-white photographs and line drawings.

Library of Congress Cataloging-in-Publication Data
Gallant, Roy A.
Private lives of the stars.
Includes index.
Summary: Discusses the major classes of stars and
describes how they are created, how they change, and
what eventually happens to them.
1. Stars—Juvenile literature.   2. Stars—Classification
—Juvenile literature.   [1. Stars] I. Title.
QB801.7.G35   1986   523.8   86-5338
ISBN 0-02-737350-9

For Elaine

Thank you to my students, many and all, who continually keep me alert by asking questions that make me challenge traditional answers that often need untraditionalizing. My special thanks to Dr. Henry Albers, friend, colleague, and astronomer at Vassar College, Poughkeepsie, New York, for checking the accuracy of this book in manuscript stage. And thanks to Phyllis Larkin, my editor, for keeping me on the track of comprehensibility and often putting me back on it when I fell off.

Contents

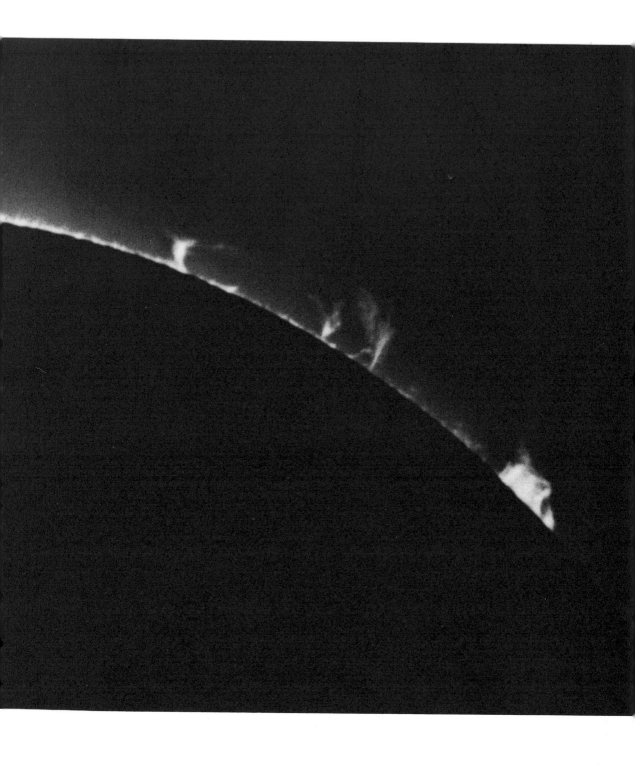

Never Take a Bite Out of the Sun

That may not sound like very sensible advice for people. But it is, for dragons, and here's why.

More than 4,000 years ago, the Chinese emperor Chung K'ang had two court astronomers named Hsi and Ho. In those days the Chinese believed that every now and then hungry dragons swept across the sky and took large bites out of the Sun. At such times the Sun would "go out" for a while. But its brightness would return if K'ang's men shouted, beat drums and heavy gongs, and shot arrows into the sky to kill the dragons. All this activity seemed to work, saving the Sun from being devoured completely. The job of Hsi and Ho was to predict when the sky dragons were going to attack the Sun so that K'ang's warriors could be ready for them. Today, of course, we know that the Sun's "going out" was nothing more than an eclipse.

An eclipsed Sun reveals its surface gases and explosive eruptions of hot gas, some arcing hundreds of thousands of miles into the Sun's thin atmosphere.
Lick Observatory

The point of the story, if you happen to be a dragon, is to stay away from the Sun or you may risk getting an arrow stuck in your tail. If you happen to be a court astronomer, the story has a different point. Even 4,000 years ago astronomers knew enough about eclipses to predict them accurately. Hsi and Ho were two such astronomers. But their fame did not last long, because one day there was an eclipse they failed to predict. Slowly the Sun began to lose its light. As the sky kept growing darker, Hsi and Ho were nowhere to be found.

In great fright, Chung K'ang called out his soldiers and ordered them to shout, beat their drums and heavy gongs, and shoot arrows into the sky to frighten away the dragons. To everyone's relief, about an hour later the Sun regained its shape and grew bright again. So all was well, except for Hsi and Ho. Emperor Chung K'ang ordered that they be killed for neglecting their duties.

Luckily, it is not as dangerous to be an astronomer today. There are no sky dragons to slay and no emperors to punish astronomers when their predictions happen to go wrong, or if they fail to make predictions at all. Now we have computers that can predict eclipses very accurately hundreds of years into the future for any position on Earth. Even so, modern astronomers do make predictions about many things that go on in the sky. We call those predictions theories. For example, they try to predict how long certain kinds of stars can go on shining before they burn out, or the future for a star like the Sun, or which of the stars we can see shining on any clear night may blow themselves to bits in gigantic explosions, or which stars may become those fascinating objects we call black holes.

So this book is about the ways astronomers today find out about the private lives of the stars: where stars come from, what makes them shine, why all stars must go out eventually, why some stars explode while others do not, and why some stars are blue, others red, and still others yellow. Those are a few of the things about stars you will learn in this book. So follow me among the stars.

Roy A. Gallant
Director/Lecturer
Southworth Planetarium
University of Southern Maine
Portland, Maine

Gods, Demons, and Fire

For as long as there have been people, they have studied the sky as a source of wonder and mystery. More than 5,000 years ago ancient stargazers, writing on blocks of clay, recorded the changing positions of the planets Mercury and Venus as they saw those planets move among the stars. They also kept records of the changing shape of the Moon as it went through phases, and of the Sun during eclipses. For those early stargazers, *any* object seen in the heavens was called a star. The planets were called wandering stars because they seemed to move among the stars. Comets were called hairy stars because of their long tails. And what we know today to be meteors were called shooting stars because they were thought to be stars falling to earth. The stars themselves were seen to flow endlessly across the heavens as a group. Because they were not seen to move about every which way like snowflakes in a blizzard, they were called fixed stars.

"The stars fell like flakes of snow," said one observer of the Leonid shower of meteors, November 13, 1833. Another observer, also believing that meteors were stars, thought that there would be no stars left in the sky the next night.

EARTH'S PLACE IN THE UNIVERSE

As we ask many questions about the universe today, so did the stargazers of old. Those questions surely included: What are the stars? Where do they come from? Are they alive? How big are they? Does Earth shine like a star? What is the place of Earth, and of the Sun, in the universe?

The answers to those questions were not to come for a very

long time. And when they did, they came slowly. At the time we are talking about—a few thousands of years ago—science did not exist. There were no chemists to explain what the stars are made of, and no physicists to explain how the stars move or how far away they are. And there were no telescopes through which to study the stars. Without science, people those many centuries ago made up stories, called myths, to explain what they saw in the sky. They made the sky a home for gods, demons, and spirits who ruled the world and were thought to control the lives of all people.

Among those who looked on the Sun as a god were New Mexico's Zuni Indians. According to Zuni creation myth, originally there were no people on Earth's surface. They were all crowded into a large, dark dungeon four levels underground. The Sun-god felt sorry for the imprisoned people, so he called his two sons to his side and said, "Let the people into the light."

The two sons went down to Earth and entered the four lower worlds. Each world became darker and darker. When the sons finally reached the people, they said, "We have come for you."

"Bring us to the Sun," the people cried.

As the people followed the two boys, their eyes hurt during the long climb to the lighter third world and the even lighter second world. "Is this the bright world where we are to live?" asked the people. "Not yet," answered the two boys.

When the people stepped out into the fresh air and bright light, they were at first blinded. The Sun's rays pained them so that tears streamed from their eyes. And as their tears mixed with the soil, buttercups and sunflowers began to grow.

"This is the world," the people said.

Try for a moment to put yourself in the place of the old star-gazers thousands of years ago. Imagine yourself studying the night sky for the first time and being asked to explain what you saw.

One thing you would most likely believe is that Earth is the center of the universe. Probably you would also say that Earth does not move in any way. Also, that the stars, Sun, and all other sky objects circle about Earth. That is what your senses would tell you.

After all, you cannot *feel* Earth move as it rotates, or spins, on its axis. The astronomer Tycho Brahe, about 300 years ago, said that Earth could not be spinning around like a top. If it did, he argued, birds would have their perches whipped out from under them. Neither can you feel Earth move as it revolves, or circles, about the Sun. And doesn't the Sun appear to rise over the same horizon each morning and set below the opposite horizon in the evening? And what about the Moon? It, too, appears to glide across the great sky dome in much the same way. Earth feels comfortably fixed and motionless in space, while all other objects seem to move around it. This is what people's senses tell them. And, after all, "seeing is believing." Or is it?

What about the height of the great sky dome? It was unknown to the stargazers of old. No one knew how to measure the height of the sky. Surely it was higher than the mountains, but how much higher no one could say. More than 2,500 years ago, people called the Babylonians built huge towering temples called ziggurats. Their tops, which reached into the sky, were supposed to be the meeting place of gods and men.

The Sumerians were an even older people who lived in what is now Iraq about 5,000 years ago. They worshiped several gods and associated the Moon, Sun, and other sky objects with those gods. Like people, the gods were thought to have personal feelings and so they had to be comforted when they became upset.

During an eclipse of the Sun, the Sun-god was thought to be

in great pain because he was being attacked by demons. The pain was worse during the first half of the eclipse as the Sun-god shone fainter and fainter. The instant an eclipse began, the priests lit a torch on the temple altar and began to say special prayers to save the fields, rivers, and other parts of the land. Meanwhile, all the people were told to cover their heads with their clothing and to shout loudly. That always seemed to end the eclipse and bring things back to normal.

Who could say that such action did not work? After all, the eclipse ended and the land and rivers were not harmed. So great was the people's fear of unusual events in the sky that few were likely to have enough courage to do nothing at all to find out if the eclipse would end on its own, instead of having to be "frightened" away.

Many clay tablets like this one made by the Sumerians and dated around 3500 B.C. consist of records of astronomical observations, showing that skywatchers were recording the changing positions of the planets, Sun, and Moon among the stars at least 5,500 years ago.

CLOUDS OF FIRE

Around 500 B.C., Greek scholars turned away from the old superstitions about the Sun, Moon, and planets being gods who ruled over all events and life on Earth. The Greeks had named the planets after their gods, as had other cultures before and after them.

Babylonian Gods	Greek Gods	Roman Gods	Role, or Association
Samash	Helios	Sol	Life, energy
Sin	Selene	Luna	Lunacy
Nabu	Hermes	Mercury	Messenger of gods
Ishtar	Aphrodite	Venus	Love and fertility
Nergal	Ares	Mars	War
Marduk	Zeus	Jupiter	King of gods
Ninib	Kronos	Saturn	Time

This new breed of scholars felt that associating the planets, stars, and other sky objects with gods was an obstacle to finding out what those objects were made of and what made them shine. They felt that they must look for natural causes, not *super*natural ones.

One such scholar thought of Earth as a flat "table" hanging in space. All the stars and planets, he said, were made from moisture rising from the ground. As the moisture rose, it became thin and changed to fire. And so the stars were born. Another Greek scholar thought of the stars as clouds that each night were set on fire and rose into the heavens. Still another also said that the stars were made of fire, and that each one rested in a bowl. At night when the stars are visible, he said, the mouths of the bowls are turned toward us and we see their fire. But during the day the bowls turn upward and hide the stars from view.

How did the Greek scholars of long ago explain, by natural causes, the nightly parade of stars across the sky? They pictured the sky dome as the upper half of a great hollow glass ball that turned slowly. Earth was at the very center and did not move. The surface of this glass ball marked the outer edge of the universe. All the stars were stuck onto its surface. Some were brighter and others dimmer, but all were the same distance from central Earth. Once a day the glass ball made one complete turn. As it did, it carried the stars around with it.

Many of the ideas of the scholars of ancient Greece seem odd to us today. But as time passed, the Greeks got better at explaining many of the things they saw in the sky. They were the first to reason that Earth is not motionless in space. They said that Earth must be spinning around like a top, and that that spinning motion makes the stars and Sun only *appear* to parade across the sky. They became the first to show that Earth was shaped like a ball instead of being flat, and they measured its size accurately. They also worked out the Moon's size and distance from Earth. The Greeks of old were the first to think that the Sun was at the center of the Solar System and that Earth and all the other planets circled the Sun. Unfortunately, however, an astronomer who lived later (Ptolemy, around A.D. 150) taught that Earth was the center of the Solar System, and that the Sun and planets all revolved about us. It took 1,500 years to correct that false view.

THE CONSTELLATIONS

If you have been to a planetarium, or have spent time finding your way around the night sky, you probably can point out two or three constellations. Constellations are groups of two or more stars that form a pattern. In some cases the pattern is easy to find, as with Orion, but in most other cases the patterns are hard to find. The constellations include dragons, giants, serpents, and other creatures in mythology. No one knows when the many constellations were invented. Most were described very long ago—by the ancient Chinese, the Mayas of Central America, the

It takes much imagination and invention to see in any constellation star group the amount of detail shown in this old representation of Orion, the Hunter.

American Indians, the Egyptians, Arabs, Greeks, and Romans.

The earliest known list of constellations was made by the Greek poet Aratus of Soli, who lived around 270 B.C. He described 44. Over the years the list has grown, so that today astronomers recognize a total of 88 "official" constellations. As we look at this or that constellation, all of its stars appear to be the same distance away from us, as if attached to the great crystal sky dome imagined by the early Greeks. Today we know that the stars making up the constellations are at many different distances from us. They are arranged in the sky not like raindrops on a window but like leaves on a tree.

So the constellations are beautifully false figures, but they are fun to find in the sky. And they are useful, as they have been for thousands of years. Navigators on land and sea once used the constellations to find their way from one distant place to another. And astronomers often use them to locate certain sky objects— for example, the Great Nebula in the constellation Orion, or the planetary nebula in the constellation Aquarius. When Halley's comet recently paid a visit, we could follow the passage of the comet through Orion, Taurus, Aries, Pisces, and Aquarius, among others.

Don't be disappointed if you can't see the constellation figures in the sky as they are pictured in books. Few people can. The constellations in our celestial zoo include nineteen land animals, thirteen humans, ten water creatures, nine birds, a couple of centaurs, one dragon, a river, a unicorn, a head of hair, and a "sea-goat," whatever that is.

As we talk about many spectacular stars and other sky objects throughout this book, we will use the constellations to find our way around the sky.

The Sun:
The Star
We Know Best

On any clear night away from city lights, you can count about 2,000 stars. With 7-power binoculars you can see more than 50,000 stars, and with a 3-inch telescope you can see hundreds of thousands. Even though the Sun's bright light masks the stars from view during the day, they are there. As the sunlight fades in the evening, the stars blink into view, twinkling as their light is disturbed by the shimmering atmosphere.

Stars are hot, glowing globes of gas that emit energy. Nearly all of a star's gas is hydrogen. Because the Sun is a hot ball of hydrogen that emits huge amounts of energy, it is a star, and the star closest to us. The next closest star is one called Alpha Centauri, more than 270,000 times farther away than the Sun.

Some stars shine mostly with red light, others mostly with yellow light, and still others mostly with bluish white light. Some are giant stars hundreds of times larger than the Sun. Others are dwarf stars many times smaller than the Sun. Some stars may be about the size of Earth, and others, called goblins, may be only the size of a pebble but weigh more than a large mountain! But such unusual stars are not known to exist for certain. They are

The ancient stargazers could not imagine the immensity of the stellar system
we now call our galaxy. Here thousands of stars are seen in the region of the
Milky Way near the constellation Cygnus. American Museum—Hayden Planetarium

among the new ideas of some astronomers. We can see some rapidly spinning stars pulse on and off like lighthouse beacons, and we can watch others swell up and shrink as they first brighten and then dim over periods lasting from a few hours to days or weeks.

Over the years astronomers have wondered if each star spends its entire "life" as the same kind of star. Or is it possible that a yellowish star like the Sun, for example, goes through different stages during its life? Perhaps it begins as a dull red star, then changes into a star that shines with a bright yellowish white light for a while, and then into still a different kind of star before it finally goes out. Astronomers have been able to answer some of those questions. And year by year they learn a bit more about the many different kinds of stars we see in the sky.

HOW FAR AWAY IS THE SUN?

At least since the time of the ancient Greeks, astronomers have known that the Sun is a star. They also knew that the Sun appears very much brighter to us than the other stars do because it is so close. But how close? Two Greek astronomers tried to figure out the distance to the Sun, but the distances they came up with were too short. One was 130 times too short, and the other was about ten times too short.

Another question they tried to answer was how big the Sun is. But without knowing its distance, they could not figure out its size. And what if all the other stars were as close to us as the Sun? Would they also appear as big, and as bright? The Greek astronomers of old couldn't agree on an answer. Some thought yes, others no.

Everything astronomers have been able to learn about the Sun and distant stars over the many years since ancient Greek times shows that the Sun, indeed, is a nearby star; it is our local star. The Sun has a family of nine known planets along with their 50 or so moons, billions of comets, and billions more of mountain-sized pieces of rock and metal called asteroids and meteoroids. Planets are solid objects (such as Earth and Mars) or large and mostly gaseous objects (such as Jupiter and Saturn) with solid centers. They do not shine with light of their own making, but with light reflected from their local star, which they circle.

All of these objects are held in orbits about the Sun by the force of gravitation, just as the Moon is held in orbit about Earth. No one knows what gravitation is, but we can measure it as a force. For instance, we know that Earth's force of gravitation is six times stronger than that of the Moon. It is stronger because Earth has more matter, or mass, packed into it as a planet than the Moon has.

Together, the Sun, planets, comets, asteroids, moons, and meteoroids make up what is called a planetary system. The name of our home planetary system is the Solar System. Other stars most likely have planetary systems also. Since there seems to be no end to the number of stars our giant telescopes keep finding, there may be billions of planets out there in the dark.

Because the Sun is the closest star, it is the easiest one to study. So the best way to begin to learn something about the other stars is to study the Sun. And that is what astronomers began to do back in the early 1600s. The Italian astronomer Galileo was the first to use a telescope to study the Sun and other stars. Since Galileo's time, astronomers have found ways to measure the Sun's distance accurately. Today we use such electronic tools as radar and artificial satellites as yardsticks.

The United States Naval Observatory in Washington, D.C., is the headquarters in this country for keeping up-to-date records of the size and distance of stars and planets. They list the "official" distance of the Sun as 149,600,000 kilometers (92,752,000 miles). Just how accurate is that figure? Distances given by different electronic instruments differ by about 3,000,000 kilometers (or about 1,860,000 miles). That seems like a lot. Because of the very large distances involved, astronomers often can't measure them as precisely as you can measure the length of your cat's tail, for example. No astronomer would argue that the Sun "actually" is a few hundred or even a few thousand kilometers more or less than 149,597,871 kilometers away. That just happens to be one precise distance measurement. For our purposes in this book, we can say that the Sun is 150 million kilometers (93 million miles) away and no one will take us to task.

HOW BIG IS THE SUN?

Until astronomers knew the Sun's distance accurately, they could not measure its size. You can understand why if you think of the size of a penny. If you hold a penny just a few inches away from your eye, it looks huge. But if you look at a penny from across a tennis court, it looks pretty small. Knowing the penny's distance is the key to finding its size. The same is true of the Sun. It turns out that the Sun's diameter, or distance across its face, is nearly 1,400,000 kilometers (865,000 miles). The Sun is so much bigger than Earth that almost 110 Earths could be lined up across the Sun's equator. Like the Sun, most of the stars we see on any clear night are enormous objects. Some are about the same size as the Sun, others are much smaller, and still others very much bigger.

What we want to do next is find out what the Sun and other stars are made of and what makes them shine. To do that, we will take an imaginary journey to the Sun, first passing through its atmosphere and then deep down into its central region, called the core.

Inside the Sun

The Sun, like a sea of flame, is never still. It is a great churning, glowing ball of gases, always changing. And its changes are what interest us most. The more we can find out about the Sun, the more we will come to know about the countless billions of other stars that lie far beyond our Solar System home.

A JOURNEY TO THE SUN—AND THROUGH THE CORONA

If we could fly to the Sun in a jet airliner traveling 1,000 kilometers (620 miles) an hour, the journey would take us about seventeen years. A *Voyager*-type space probe would get us there in about half a year. But if we traveled at the speed of light, we would make the trip in only eight minutes. The speed of light is 300,000 kilometers (186,000 miles) a second.

The Sun's feathery top layer of atmosphere, called the corona, is not visible from Earth because Earth's atmosphere masks it out. But the corona is visible from space. Corona means "crown."

The Sun's corona streams far out into space as a delicate feathery halo visible to us only during a solar eclipse, or through special telescopes used at large observatories. NASA

We find that the gases of the corona are like those of the Sun itself—mostly hydrogen, along with some helium and small amounts of heavier gases. Of the more than 100 chemical elements, hydrogen is the lightest and has the simplest atoms. (Atoms are the tiniest possible amounts of an element. For example, an atom of gold is the smallest possible piece of gold.) A hydrogen atom has one tiny central particle called a proton. Another particle, called an electron and even smaller, moves about the proton. That is all there is to a hydrogen atom.

Helium is the second lightest and simplest chemical element. It is the gas that makes a circus balloon lighter than air. A helium atom has two protons along with two other particles called neutrons in its central region. Two electrons move about the proton-neutron core.

The hydrogen and helium atoms that make up the feathery sea

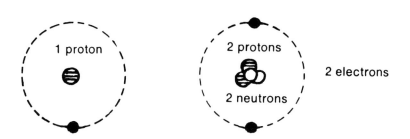

Hydrogen (*left*) is the simplest element, having a single proton forming its nucleus, and one orbital electron. The atom is held together by the positive charge of the proton and the negative charge of the electron attracting each other. Helium (*right*) is the second simplest atom, having two protons and two neutrons forming the nucleus and two orbital electrons. Since neutrons do not have an electrical charge, the two negative electrons are "balanced" by the two positive protons. Notice that hydrogen lacks neutrons.

of the corona are darting about very swiftly. Scientists measure their speed as temperature on a special temperature scale called the Kelvin scale. The temperature of the corona is 1,000,000 kelvins (degrees). (A kelvin is a degree of temperature used by astronomers to measure the temperature of stars. Room temperature in kelvin degrees is about 300. On your living-room thermometer, that is 68 degrees Fahrenheit.)

We notice that bright streaks of light flash out from the Sun and make the corona shimmer. Another thing we notice is that tufts of gas stream out from opposite sides of the Sun. This shows that, like Earth, the Sun has a north and a south magnetic pole. Magnetism, it turns out, plays an important part in the Sun's activity, just as it does in Earth's. Because the strength of the Sun's magnetism changes from place to place on its surface, from day to day and from month to month, no two photographs of the corona are ever exactly alike.

Every second countless trillions of stray protons and electrons are cast off by the Sun. They shoot out through the corona and out through the Solar System as the solar wind. This wind of atomic particles blows over all the planets. One effect on Earth is the grand display of Northern Lights that we see from time to time. On Earth we are protected by the shield of the atmosphere from this solar bombardment. Without that protection from this hail of solar particles, or the protection of space suits during our imaginary journey to the Sun, we would be broiled like grilled steaks. The hail of energy grows even stronger as we move nearer the Sun.

We now decide to increase our speed to 160,000 kilometers (100,000 miles) a second. That will bring us close to the Sun in a little more than fifteen minutes. By that time we find ourselves deep inside the Sun's lower atmosphere. It is called the chromosphere, which means "color sphere."

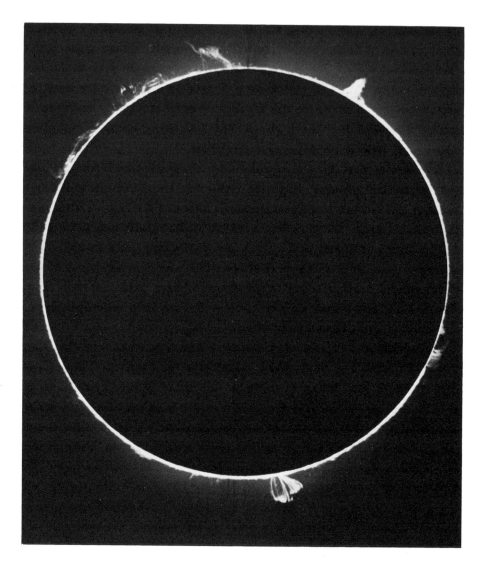

With special attachments to their telescopes, astronomers can block out the Sun's blazingly bright disk and photograph fiery loops of gas and other explosive features, called prominences, in the Sun's surface gases. Some prominences leap up out of the Sun to heights of hundreds of thousands of miles.

Mount Wilson and Las Campanas Observatories, Carnegie Institution of Washington

INTO THE CHROMOSPHERE

The chromosphere is sandwiched between the corona and the Sun's surface layer of gases. When the Sun is in eclipse, the chromosphere appears as a narrow but bright pinkish rim around the blacked-out Sun, a deeper color than the corona.

The chromosphere stretches out some 2,500 kilometers (1,550 miles) from the Sun's surface. It is a deep layer of raging gases where huge tongues of hot gas leap 10,000 kilometers (6,200 miles) high. Called spicules, meaning "little spikes," they shoot up from enormous boiling cells of gas below. Each cell measures some 1,000 kilometers (600 miles) across.

Great loops of hot gases break up through the chromosphere from time to time and arch to heights of 100,000 kilometers (62,000 miles) or more. They are called prominences. The chromosphere also lights up with violent flash explosions called flares. Flares range in size from a few kilometers to several thousand kilometers wide and may last from a few minutes to an hour or so. These storms cast off streams of pieces of atoms that feed the solar wind. A single flare may give off the energy of 10 million hydrogen bombs! When the Sun is especially active, flares explode every hour or so. They are the cause of the Northern Lights mentioned earlier.

Depending on the activity of the chromosphere, its temperature varies from a low of about 4,500 kelvins to about 50,000 kelvins.

THE SUN'S SOFT "SURFACE"

The Sun's surface is not solid. Instead, it is a boiling sea of hot gases called the photosphere, meaning "light sphere." The temperature of this layer is about 6,000 kelvins.

Hot, swelling mountains of gases called granules keep the photosphere churning, like a tub of bubbling tar. Dark patches called sunspots come and go among the granules. They seem to be caused by magnetism within deeper layers of the Sun's gases.

Like other stars, the Sun's surface is composed of hot gases, here seen shining with the light given off by hydrogen, which gives the surface gases a granular appearance. The white dot at lower right represents Earth's size compared with the much larger Sun. Mount Wilson and Las Campanas Observatories, Carnegie Institution of Washington

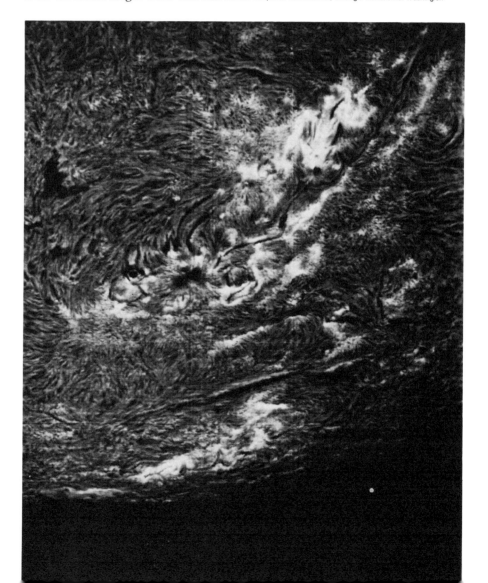

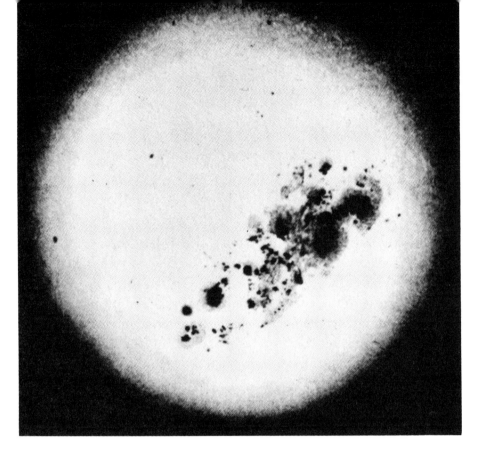

Sunspots occur in regular cycles and are associated with an "active" Sun. Most of these upwellings of hot gases appear about a third of the way between the Sun's equator and poles and have a life of a few hours to several days.

Sunspots appear dark in photographs because their gases well up and cool. As they cool, they turn darker than the hotter surrounding gases lower down. A typical sunspot is about the size of Earth.

Photographs taken of a group of sunspots over a period of several days show that the spots move across the Sun's surface. Because they are rooted in the photosphere, their motion means that the Sun's surface gases are being carried around by the Sun's rotation on its axis. Following their motion tells us that the Sun rotates once every 27 days. Sunspots come and go in cycles of about every eleven years. The next active sunspot period will be in 1991–92.

INTO THE SUN'S CENTER

What makes the Sun and other stars shine? Years ago people thought the Sun was a huge ball of fire. They thought that the other stars also were flaming objects. Today we know that cannot be so. Why? Because a lump of coal the size of the Sun, or a Sun-sized ball of wood, could burn for only a few thousand years before nothing would be left but ash. Astronomers have good reasons to think that the Sun has been shining for nearly 5 billion years. That is very much longer than only a few thousand years.

Also, a star is too hot to burn. That may sound strange, but it is so. Gases on Earth are made up of whole atoms. With enough heat, the whole atoms of a piece of wood or paper join with oxygen atoms in the air in the process we call combustion, or burning. But the atoms of the Sun's gases are moving about so fast, and smashing into each other so hard, that they break apart into their individual protons, electrons, and neutrons. So there are no whole atoms of anything on the Sun. That means that burning cannot take place. The Sun must produce its huge outpouring of energy in a way other than burning.

To find out how the Sun produces its energy, we must travel right down into the core. There we find a huge pool of individual protons packed very tightly together and smashing into each other with tremendous force. The temperature in the core is about 15 million kelvins. As those protons collide, they fuse, or stick together. Each fusion releases a small amount of energy, but there are billions upon billions of fusions going on each second, so huge amounts of energy are produced. After a certain number of fusions, a clump of protons is built up. Some of the protons are changed into neutrons, and the core of a helium atom is formed.

So the cores of hydrogen atoms (protons) fuse and form the cores (protons and neutrons) of helium atoms. It is this process of fusion of hydrogen into helium that is the source of energy of the Sun, and of other stars.

The Sun's core is so tightly packed with hydrogen and helium that it takes a small burst of fusion energy 50 million years to work its way up to the Sun's surface. But it then takes that energy only eight minutes to cross the 150-million-kilometer distance of space to Earth. That is because all the energy produced in the Sun travels at the speed of light once it breaks free of the Sun. That energy then reaches us on Earth in many forms—including light, heat, X rays, and the ultraviolet waves that cause "sunburn."

It takes only a very small amount of hydrogen to produce a very large amount of energy. Because stars are such massive objects made of so much hydrogen, they can go on pouring out energy, or shining, for thousands, millions, or billions of years before using up their hydrogen fuel supply. From what we can tell about the Sun, it has been shining for about 5 billion years. Astronomers tell us that it has enough hydrogen fuel left to keep it shining for about another 5 billion years. But as each star eventually must use up the last of its fuel, it must stop shining and die. Some do so quietly. Others do so in catastrophic explosions. Before we find out how these stars blow themselves to bits, we must first ask where the Sun and other stars came from. How were they formed?

It All Started with a BIG BANG!

It was the most fantastic explosion anyone can imagine. What was to become every piece of matter in the universe was packed into a tiny pinpoint of mass, a kind of super-atom. Sometime between 12 billion and 20 billion years ago, that super-atom exploded in what astronomers call the Big Bang.

The fireball explosion of the Big Bang sent matter flying off in all directions. At that moment, time and the universe began. The universe has been expanding, or growing larger, ever since.

THE FIRST KINDS OF MATTER

Just after the explosion, nearly all of the universe was a hot cloud of hydrogen. Over the next several seconds, some of the hydrogen fused and formed helium, just as happens today in the hot core of the Sun and other stars. Then over the next minute or so, as the young universe kept expanding, the hydrogen was spread out too thinly for more fusions to take place. So in only a few minutes after the universe began, nine-tenths of it was hydrogen and one-tenth had become helium.

THE GALAXIES FORM

We now move forward in time to about 100,000 to a million years after the Big Bang. By this time the hydrogen and helium had collected into giant clouds. These clouds of mostly hydrogen were the early stages of the many galaxies—those vast cities of stars that we see all over the sky today. In the early stages of the galaxies, we can imagine some parts of a galaxy-cloud having large and dense collections of matter, and other parts having only small amounts of matter spread out thinly. Today our giant telescopes show us billions of galaxies. All seem to be from about 10 billion to 15 billion years old, more than twice the age of the Sun.

STARS BEGIN TO FORM

Each new galaxy-cloud contained millions of smaller cloud clumps of mostly hydrogen along with some helium. These "smaller" clouds—many millions of kilometers across—became the birthplace of stars. We can imagine some of the bigger clouds with lots of mass, or matter, attracting and swallowing up less massive clouds nearby. The more massive a cloud, the stronger its gravity, its ability to pull surrounding matter into itself.

Again, although no one knows what gravity is, we know how it acts. For example, the more massive any two objects are, the stronger is their gravitational attraction for each other. And the closer any two objects are, the stronger is their attraction for each other. So large objects in space near each other, such as Earth and the Moon, attract each other more strongly than smaller objects that are far apart, such as the two moons of Mars.

As a hydrogen cloud grew even bigger by collecting still more matter, its gravity caused the cloud to tumble in on itself. The cloud's hydrogen was packed tighter and tighter, especially in the

From a great distance in space our home galaxy, the Milky Way, would resemble this view of the Andromeda Galaxy some two million light-years distant. The two bright objects are smaller companion galaxies. The smaller dots are stars belonging to our galaxy. Palomar Observatory core region of the cloud. Whenever matter is packed in this way it heats up, just as a bicycle pump heats up when you pump (compress) gas into a tire. Because the core region of a star is packed most tightly with gas, it heats up much more than the regions near and at the surface where the gases are not very dense.

Many globules, which are dark concentrations of matter thought to be the first stage of star formation, can be seen in this section of the Rosette Nebula.
Palomar Observatory

So the cores of the millions of star-clouds forming in all the young galaxies grew hotter and hotter as the matter of each cloud kept falling into the core region and packing itself more densely, or tightly.

At first, a young star-cloud, called a protostar, glows a dull red from the heat produced in its core. As the protostar grows still hotter, it begins to shine a bright cherry red. Then when the core temperature zooms to about 10 million kelvins, the young star begins to fuse hydrogen into helium. This new source of energy causes the star to shine with a hotter yellowish white light. The hottest stars of all shine with a bluish white light.

Color, then, is a key to learning how hot an object is. If you hold a poker in a blazing fire long enough, the poker heats up. As it does, it glows a dull red at first; then as it grows hotter it shines a bright cherry red. If you next fan the fire around the poker, the poker heats up even more and becomes white-hot. A still hotter fire would turn the poker bluish white before melting it.

DWARFS AND GIANTS

For now, it is important to know why some stars in midlife are red, others yellowish white, and still others bluish white. We could rephrase that and ask why all stars in midlife are not the same color. The answer is that color is determined by the temperature of the surface layers of the star's gases, which in turn is determined by how hot it gets in the core. And that eventually is determined by the amount of matter the original star-cloud had when the star was formed.

Stars like the Sun form out of hydrogen clouds with enough matter to tumble into the core region and heat the core up to about 15 million kelvins. That is hot enough to make the surface of Sunlike stars shine with a yellowish white light. A star that forms out of a hydrogen cloud with only about one-tenth as much matter as the Sun cannot raise its core temperature to much more than 10 million kelvins. Such stars are rather small and cool red stars, called red dwarfs. The core of a star that forms out of a hydrogen cloud with about ten times more matter than a Sunlike star-cloud heats up to about 50 million kelvins. These extremely hot stars shine with a bluish white light and are very much larger than the Sun. We call them blue giants and supergiants. They are the superstars of the universe.

THE NEBULAE:
THE BIRTHPLACE OF STARS

Stars are still forming today in many parts of our galaxy, and in the other galaxies as well. The birthplaces of stars are those huge clouds of gas and dust called nebulae that we see throughout the Milky Way and other galaxies. They are gas clouds left over from the time of the Big Bang, and other such clouds made up of gases cast off by aging stars. The gas of the nebulae is mostly hydrogen with some helium. The "dust" is made up of tiny particles of solid matter that formed along with the first stars.

Some nebulae are called dark nebulae because they appear as dark patches outlined by the light of stars shining behind them. The famous Horsehead Nebula in the constellation Orion, the Hunter, is one of the most spectacular dark nebulae. It is seen just below the lowest of Orion's three belt stars.

When a cloud of gas and dust has one or more stars inside it, or nearby, the nebula may reflect the light from those stars. These are called reflection nebulae. The beautiful Pleiades star cluster contains several reflection nebulae. It is seen just above the V-shaped face of the constellation Taurus, the Bull.

If the star or stars inside a nebula heat the gas to about 10,000 kelvins, the hydrogen of the nebula is energized, or excited, and glows like a fluorescent light bulb. Nebulae that give off light in this way are called emission nebulae. The most famous one is the Great Nebula seen in Orion. It is the middle star of Orion's sword

Right: The Horsehead Nebula, one of the most splendid visible to us, is an example of a dark nebula. We see this great dark cloud of gas and dust outlined by light emitted from stars on the far side of the nebula. Mount Wilson and Las Campanas Observatories, Carnegie Institution of Washington

Below: The Great Nebula in the constellation Orion is an example of an emission nebula, one whose gas re-emits the energy of nearby hot blue stars. Mount Wilson and Las Campanas Observatories, Carnegie Institution of Washington

and can be found with binoculars. It appears as a bright greenish mist through a small telescope. When photographed with a large telescope, it is one of the most beautiful objects in the heavens— a great glowing cloud that suggests what the universe may have been like early in its creation. One astronomer has described the Great Nebula as resembling a giant ghostly bat. There is enough gas and dust in the Great Nebula to form 3,000 stars like the Sun.

Remember that it is the amount of matter that an individual star-cloud manages to collect into itself that determines what kind of a star the new star will become. The more matter a star-cloud has, the more massive, bigger, and hotter the new star will be.

It's time now for us to take a closer look into the private lives of the stars. We will begin with the giants of the heavens.

Superstars:
The Blue Giants
and White Giants

The fact that we call certain stars giants or supergiants, and certain other stars dwarfs, suggests that there is a big difference in size among the stars. And so there is. But how do we *know*? No matter what its size, each distant star appears to us only as a pinpoint of light. It makes no difference whether we view the stars through binoculars, a small telescope, or a large one. All the stars appear to be the same size—only pinpoints of light. But some of those pinpoints appear dazzlingly bright, while others appear dim.

FINDING THE SIZE OF STARS

To find out the size of stars other than the Sun, astronomers closely study the color of the star whose size they want to know. On any clear night, when your eyes have adjusted to the darkness for about 20 minutes, you can see, even without binoculars or a telescope, that some stars are reddish, others are pale yellow, and still others bluish white. For example, in the constellation Orion, the star at the upper left and marking one shoulder of the giant is reddish, and the one at the lower right and marking his knee is bluish. Astronomers have special attachments for their telescopes that enable them to measure a star's color with great accuracy.

Remember what we said in the last chapter about how the color of a star tells us how hot the star is? A yellowish white star like the Sun has a surface temperature of about 6,000 kelvins. A cool reddish star has a surface temperature of about 3,000 kelvins. Suppose now that we are looking at two stars, both red. Both appear only as pinpoints of light, but one appears much brighter than the other. We look up each star in special books, prepared by astronomers, that give information about the star's brightness, type, and distance, for example. We find that both stars are about the same distance away. We can now deduce that the brighter of the two stars must be pouring out more energy than the dimmer one. (The amount of energy any star pours out is called its luminosity.) We also deduce that the more luminous of the two stars must also be the larger one.

Why? Think of it this way. A patch of the dimmer star's surface gases one meter square is pouring out exactly the same amount of light-energy as a surface patch the same size on the brighter star. That has to be so because the red color of both stars tells us that each has a surface temperature of 3,000 kelvins. The only way one star can be brighter than the other is for the brighter one to have a larger surface from which to pour out more light—in other words, to be bigger.

THE BLUE GIANTS, WHITE GIANTS, AND SUPERGIANTS

The most massive stars, and some of the largest stars, we see shining in the night sky are the blue and white giants and supergiants. Among the many we know are Rigel, in Orion; Deneb, in Cygnus, the Swan; and the beautiful stars that make up the Pleiades.

It is important here to review the difference between "mass" and "size." Mass, remember, is the amount of matter an object contains. Size is the space that the mass fills. We can have a very large star with not very much mass, if that mass is spread out thinly within the star. And we can have another star the same size, but with much more mass packed into it. We then say that the second star is more massive than the first one. We will come across such differences later.

The blue and white giants and supergiants may be hundreds of times larger and more massive than the Sun, and blaze away with many thousands of times more light and other energy. Their surface gases have temperatures around 50,000 kelvins, eight times more than the Sun's surface gases. And their core temperatures are more than 20 million kelvins, compared with the Sun's core temperature of about 15 million kelvins.

Because the core temperatures of the blue-white supergiants are so high, these stars are element factories on a grand scale. As mentioned earlier, medium-mass stars like the Sun produce enough heat in their cores to fuse hydrogen into helium. (Recall that hydrogen is the lightest chemical element and helium the second lightest. Other elements are still heavier. After helium come lithium, beryllium, boron, carbon, nitrogen, oxygen, and so on, each heavier than the one before.) If a star's core heats up to more than the core of the Sun, the temperatures will be high enough to cause helium to fuse into the heavier element carbon. It turns out that medium-mass stars like the Sun do fuse helium into carbon, but they usually cannot produce elements heavier than carbon.

Since the blue and white giants and supergiants have very high core temperatures, they are able to fuse helium into carbon, and carbon into the still heavier element iron. But elements heavier than iron are not produced by stars during the main part of their lives. The blue and white giants and supergiants are so hot that they use up the hydrogen fuel supply in their cores much faster than Sunlike stars do. So the life spans of these very massive stars are only several millions of years, a short time compared with the ten-billion-year life span of cooler Sunlike stars. Astronomers base their estimates of the life spans of stars on the amount of hydrogen fuel a star has, divided by the rate at which the hydrogen is being used up.

As you will find later, these giant stars sometimes end their lives in gigantic explosions. For now, all we need remember about them is that they have lots of mass, are very large, very hot, and have the shortest life spans of all stars. A close look into the personal lives of a few of these stars will show some fascinating things about them.

RIGEL—A BLUE SUPERGIANT

Rigel is the seventh brightest star in the sky and marks the left leg of Orion. The star's name comes from the Arabic *Rijl Jauzah al Yusra,* which means the "left leg of the giant." You can easily see Rigel just by looking at Orion. In fact, the star calls attention to itself with its brilliance. It is a distant star about 900 light-years away and appears bluish white.

Rigel's surface gases are twice as hot as the Sun's, but the star pours out thousands of times more energy than the Sun does and is one of the most fiercely shining stars in our galaxy. Rigel is so large that if it replaced the Sun as our local star it would spread out beyond Mercury. It also is an especially massive star.

If you studied Rigel through a telescope, you would see that it is not one star, but two. Such stars are called double stars, or

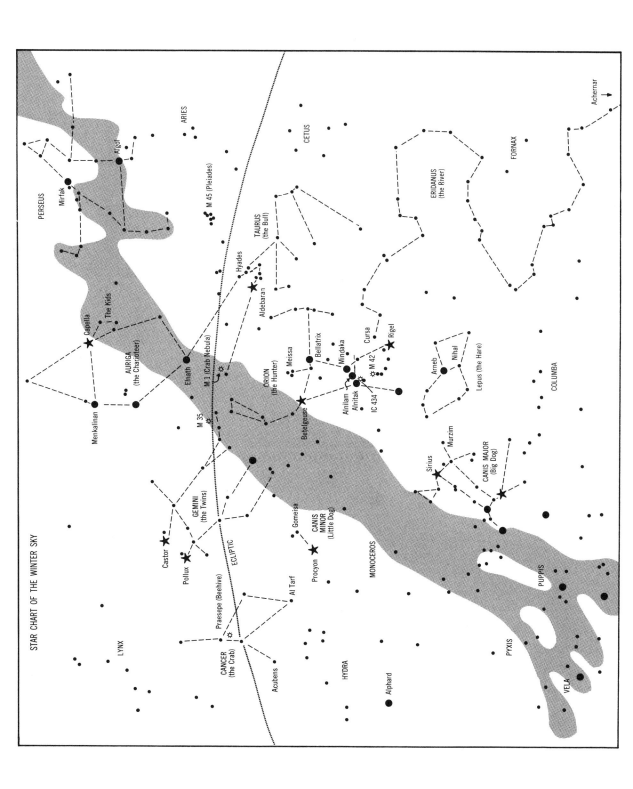

STAR CHART OF THE WINTER SKY

PERSEUS
Mirfak
Algol
ARIES
CETUS
FORNAX
M 45 (Pleiades)
ERIDANUS (the River)
Achernar
Capella
The Kids
AURIGA (the Charioteer)
Elnath
Hyades
Aldebaran
TAURUS (the Bull)
Menkalinan
M 1 (Crab Nebula)
M 35
Meissa
Bellatrix
Mindaka
Cursa
Rigel
Arneb
Nihal
Lepus (the Hare)
COLUMBA
ORION (the Hunter)
Betelgeuse
Alnilam
Alnitak
M 42
IC 434
Murzim
Sirius
CANIS MAJOR (Big Dog)
Castor
Pollux
GEMINI (the Twins)
Gomeisa
CANIS MINOR (Little Dog)
Procyon
MONOCEROS
PUPPIS
LYNX
Praesepe (Beehive)
Al Tarf
ECLIPTIC
PYXIS
CANCER (the Crab)
Acubens
HYDRA
Alphard
VELA

binary stars. They circle a common center, about once every 50 years, the way the two ends of a dumbbell would if you spun it around. About half the stars in the sky are double stars. The main star of Rigel is called Rigel A, and its companion is called Rigel B. Rigel B itself is a double star, the two stars taking nearly ten days to circle each other. That is a very short time compared with other binary stars. Rigel B appears as a small bluish star just about as bright as Rigel A.

Portrait of Rigel

Surface temperature: 12,000 kelvins
Energy output: 150,000 times more than the Sun
Diameter: 50 times larger than the Sun
Mass: 50 times more massive than the Sun
Distance: 900 light-years

Rigel is the brightest star among a large group of blue giants seen in the region near Orion. Rigel must be a very young star that is shining so brightly that it cannot last for more than a few million more years.

A SUPERGIANT PUZZLE

One of the more fascinating stars in the sky is the third brightest star in the constellation Auriga, the Charioteer. It sits high above Orion in the winter sky. As a constellation, Auriga has a history older than most. There is nothing in its shape to remind us of a chariot or a charioteer, but down through the ages the Babylonians, Greeks, Arabs, and even the faraway Chinese have all associated this constellation with a chariot. Just as puzzling is why the charioteer should be carrying a full-grown goat on his shoulder along with three baby goats, or kids, in one arm.

The star that interests us in this constellation is the one called Epsilon Aurigae. It is just to the right of and below Capella, the constellation's brightest star. Epsilon Aurigae is the top star in that small triangle of three stars known as "the kids." It is a distant star some 2,000 light-years away and may be about 200 times larger, and about 20 times more massive, than the Sun. It is a hot supergiant that may outshine Rigel with the energy output of about 60,000 Suns.

Portrait of Epsilon Aurigae

Surface temperature: a bit hotter than the Sun
Energy output: 60,000 times more than the Sun
Diameter: 200 times larger than the Sun
Mass: about 20 times more massive than the Sun
Distance: 2,000 light-years

Epsilon Aurigae is what astronomers call an eclipsing binary star. That means that it is a double star whose companion from time to time eclipses, or blocks out, the light of Epsilon Aurigae as the two stars circle each other. Whenever the dim companion glides past and in front of the bright main star, it blocks out part of the main star's light and to us its brightness appears to dim. After the pass is completed, we see the binary pair as bright as before. Sometimes there is a second dimming when the companion star circles behind the main star so that *its* light is dimmed or cut off completely.

Such eclipses of Epsilon Aurigae by its companion take place once every 27 years. Knowing the size of the companion's orbit and that it takes the companion 27 years to complete one orbit tells us the distance separating the two stars—about 4.5 billion kilometers (2.8 billion miles). That is about 30 times the Sun's distance from Earth.

The fascinating thing about Epsilon Aurigae is its mysterious companion. For one thing, no one has ever seen it. But from what astronomers can tell, it may be a super-supergiant, possibly the largest and coolest star known—if it is a star at all. Right now, it is probably safer to refer to it simply as an "object." Its temperature seems to be a cool 500 kelvins, which means that the object is not hot enough to give off light. Its mass seems to be about sixteen times that of the Sun, but its size may be fifteen times greater than Epsilon Aurigae. If it took the Sun's place, it would fill out the Solar System almost to Saturn's orbit. Quite a "star." So much matter spread out so thinly within the object means that it is nearly a perfect vacuum, something like the thin tail of a comet. Even so, the object has enough matter so that when it crosses in front of Epsilon Aurigae it dims Epsilon Aurigae to about half its usual brightness.

Some astronomers think that the companion is a huge disk of gas, dust, and solid particles whirling around a pair of small stars that we cannot see. Jets of gas may be shooting out of the disk from opposite surfaces of the central disk. Possibly a planetary system is beginning to form at the disk's center. Maybe it is this disk of matter that eclipses Epsilon Aurigae once every 27 years. The last such eclipse took place between 1982 and 1984. The next one is scheduled between 2009 and 2011. No matter what the explanation turns out to be, Epsilon Aurigae and its mystery companion will continue to be among the most fascinating stars.

DENEB—THE SWAN STAR

According to myth, the musician-king of the Ligurians, who long ago lived in an area between Italy and France, had a friend who was killed. So great was his grief for his dead friend that he thought he, too, would die. The god Apollo took pity and spared the musician-king further grief by raising him among the stars as Cygnus, the Swan. Ever since then, swans are said to sing sad songs when they are about to die, hence our expression "swan song." The constellation Cygnus also is known as the Northern Cross, since the swan's outstretched wings cross a line drawn between its head and tail stars.

Portrait of Deneb

Surface temperature: 9,700 kelvins
Energy output: 100,000 times more than the Sun
Diameter: 60 times larger than the Sun
Mass: 25 times more massive than the Sun
Distance: 2,300 light-years

If you find the constellation Cygnus, the Swan, and locate its brightest star, Deneb, you will see one of the greatest hot supergiant stars known. Deneb is the nineteenth-brightest star in the sky. It marks the tail of the swan who is seen flying down along that part of the Milky Way visible to us in the Northern

Hemisphere in summer and is the faintest of the three stars forming the well-known Summer Triangle—Deneb, Vega, and Altair. Deneb's name comes from the Arabic *Al Dhanab,* which means "the hen's tail."

With a surface temperature of 9,700 kelvins, Deneb shines with an intense white light. It is brighter than about 100,000 Suns, which puts it in a class with Rigel and Epsilon Aurigae. Deneb probably has about 25 times more mass than the Sun and a diameter about 60 times as great. At a distance of about 2,300 light-years, the star is one of the most distant of the brighter stars visible to us.

THE SEVEN SISTERS

Riding high above the V-shaped head of the constellation Taurus, the Bull, is the most beautiful cluster of stars that can be seen by the naked eye. They are called the Pleiades, or the Seven Sisters (see page 00). Astronomers call this and other such star groups galactic clusters. As part of Taurus, the Pleiades are seen from the Northern Hemisphere in the fall and winter sky to the right of and just above Orion. The Pleiades have long been associated with the time of death, since they reach their highest point in the sky in November, when it turns cold and the land is dry and lifeless. But they also have been associated with rebirth and life. When they are seen to rise in the east at the time of sunrise, they announce the arrival of spring, a time when the land once again comes alive.

The Pleiades are an example of a reflection nebula, one whose dust reflects the light of one or more stars embedded in the nebula. Lick Observatory

There are many myths about the Pleiades—North and South American Indian, Chinese, Polynesian, and Greek, to name a few. According to one Greek myth, the Pleiades were seven daughters of the creator-god, Atlas, and his wife, Pleione. It is said that Zeus, king of the gods, elevated them to stardom when they died of grief over the death of their half-sisters, the Hyades.

You can see the Pleiades as a tight little group of six or seven stars, depending on your eyesight and how clear the sky is. But there are probably at least 500 stars in this group. On viewing them through binoculars, the astronomer Robert Burnham, Jr., described them as follows: "In a dark sky the eight or nine bright members glitter like an array of icy blue diamonds on black velvet; a frosty impression is given by a nebulous haze which swirls about the stars and reflects their gleaming radiance like pale moonlight on a field of snow crystals."

Portrait of Alcyone

Surface temperature: 30,000 kelvins
Energy output: 1,000 times more than the Sun
Diameter: 10 times larger than the Sun
Mass: (not known)
Distance: 410 light-years

The nine brightest stars in the Pleiades are all hot blue giants about 410 light-years away. The brightest star in the group—the central star, Alcyone—is about ten times the Sun's size and 1,000 times brighter. The stars of the Pleiades seem to be young stars only about 50 million years old, formed after the dinosaurs became extinct. The entire swarm is wrapped within a haze thought to be gas, dust, and solid particles left over from the time the stars formed. A time-exposure photograph through a telescope shows much detail of the Pleiades nebula, which has been described as looking like "a breath on a mirror."

ZETA PUPPIS AND SIRIUS

Before examining a few of the cool red giant and supergiant stars, we should take a look at two more of the very hot blue-white superbeacons of the sky. The first is Zeta Puppis, the brightest star in the constellation Puppis, meaning the stern (of a ship). It is located just below and to the left of the constellation Canis Major. Zeta Puppis is a bluish white supergiant and in brightness ranks with Rigel and Deneb, which makes it one of the most energetic stars in our galaxy. It does not appear as bright to the eye, however, due to its great distance of 2,400 light-years.

Portrait of Zeta Puppis

Surface temperature: 35,000 kelvins
Energy output: 60,000 times more than the Sun
Diameter: (not known)
Mass: (not known)
Distance: 2,400 light-years

The last of the hot superstars we will mention is by no means the least. In fact, it is the brightest star in the sky, except for the Sun. The star is Sirius, in the constellation Canis Major, or the

Great Dog, one of Orion's two hunting dogs. Canis Major is just behind and below Orion. You can easily find Sirius by following a line down through Orion's three belt stars. All winter long in the Northern Hemisphere Sirius dominates the night sky. The star rises around nine in the evening near Thanksgiving, and around seven at Christmas.

Sirius is the fifth-nearest known star, less than nine light-years away. Considering its closeness, and that it is 23 times more energetic than the Sun, you can understand why the star blazes away so brightly. Although a giant in brightness, it is not a giant in size. It is just less than twice the Sun's size and has a little more than twice the Sun's mass. Its surface temperature is about 10,000 kelvins.

Portrait of Sirius

Surface temperature: 10,000 kelvins
Energy output: 23 times more than the Sun
Diameter: twice the Sun's size
Mass: twice the Sun's mass
Distance: 9 light-years

The name Sirius comes from a Greek word meaning "sparkling," or "scorching." The ancient Egyptians associated their goddess Isis with Sirius. When Sirius was seen to rise just before dawn, around June 25, the Egyptians knew that the yearly flooding of the great river Nile would soon begin. That was the signal for farmers to start planting their crops. So Sirius's rising with the Sun marked an important time for all life in Egypt. That season also brought the heat of summer, which superstitious people thought drove dogs mad. For that reason Sirius was nicknamed the Dog Star. The ancient Chinese associated not a dog but a wolf with this star group.

Sirius, too, is a double star. Its companion, Sirius B, is a very small star, a dwarf star nicknamed the Pup. The two stars circle each other once every 50 years. From what you have found out about stars so far, think for a moment about these facts about Sirius B, the Pup: It has just about as much mass as the Sun. It has a surface temperature of about 9,000 kelvins (that is, 3,000 kelvins hotter than the Sun). Its diameter is 50 times *smaller* than the Sun's. That makes the star only a little more than twice Earth's size! Two questions you now might consider are these: 1. Is Sirius B a brightly shining star, or a dim star? 2. Compared with a teaspoonful of the Sun's matter, would a teaspoonful of Sirius B's matter weigh less or more?

We will return to these questions and Sirius B in the chapter about dwarf stars. It is now time to examine some of the red giants and supergiants mentioned earlier.

More Superstars: The Red Giants

Stars do not remain the same throughout their lives. Like a moth, which begins as an egg, then lives a while as a caterpillar, then spins a cocoon and further develops as a pupa, and finally emerges as a colorful adult winged moth, a star goes through various stages in its life history. Recall that a star like the Sun begins as a dim red object and then, as its core heats up, shines with a yellowish white light, which is the stage the Sun is in today. But one day, when the Sun uses up its hydrogen fuel supply, it will enter a different stage, swelling up and for a time shining as a red giant star. For reasons we will describe later, it will then shrink and become a very small dwarf star, shining with an intense white light. The white and bluish white giant stars described in the previous chapter also go through different stages as they use up their hydrogen fuel and become red giant stars, but in their case they become red supergiants because of their large amount of mass.

BETELGEUSE—A RED SUPERGIANT

From what astronomers know about stars, the red giant or supergiant stage marks the beginning of the end of a star's life. The bright red star marking one of Orion's shoulders is a red supergiant called Betelgeuse. The name comes from two Arabic words, *Beit Algueze,* and means "the armpit of the giant." Betelgeuse, one of the most famous of all the red giants and supergiants, is the eleventh-brightest star and can be seen from most places on Earth. It is about 520 light-years away, not especially distant, and has a diameter a few hundred times that of the Sun.

Portrait of Betelgeuse

Surface temperature: 3,100 kelvins
Energy output: 14,000 times more than the Sun
Diameter: 500 times larger than the Sun
Mass: 20 times that of the Sun
Distance: 520 light-years

Betelgeuse probably started out as a massive blue giant or supergiant like Rigel and Deneb. For tens of thousands, or tens of millions, of years it continued to shine by fusing hydrogen into helium. But as it used up the last of its hydrogen fuel, the core region of the star cooled. Soon there was no longer enough heat in its nuclear furnace to support the great weight of the surface gases pressing down from above. Those gases then came crashing down into the core region. As they did, the core quickly became very hot again, hot enough to start new nuclear reactions. This new source of energy from the collapse of the star pushed the star's gases outward, causing it to swell up as a red supergiant. The time from "normal" star to red supergiant probably took about 20,000 years. Because the gases in a puffed-up red supergiant are spread out so thinly, these stars have been called "red-hot vacuums."

Betelgeuse is a variable star. (We will take a closer look at these interesting stars in Chapter 8.) A variable star is one that swells up, then shrinks, then swells up again in cycles of days, weeks, months, or years, depending on the star in question. Betelgeuse grows from largest to smallest and then back to largest again about once every six years. The star becomes dimmer as it shrinks, then brighter as it grows larger. When at its brightest and biggest, Betelgeuse shines with the light of 14,000 Suns, about twice as brightly as when it is dimmest.

At its dimmest and smallest, Betelgeuse is about 500 times larger than the Sun. If Betelgeuse, when at that size, took the Sun's place as our local star, it would swallow up Mercury, Venus, Earth, and fill up the Solar System out to the orbit of Mars. At its largest, it is about 920 times bigger than the Sun and would fill up the Solar System possibly out to the orbit of Jupiter.

ANTARES—AN EVIL SUPERGIANT

The constellation Scorpius, the Scorpion, also has an impressive red supergiant star, the one named Antares. In mythology, Scorpius was considered an evil creature. Orion, the Hunter, had boasted that so great was his skill that, if he wanted to, he could kill all the animals on Earth. On hearing of his boast, the Earth goddess, Gaea, was fearful that he might actually do just that. So she sent Scorpius to sting Orion to death, which the scorpion did. Both Orion and Scorpius were then given places in the sky,

STAR CHART OF THE SUMMER SKY

BOÖTES

Nusakan
Alphecca
CORONA BOREALIS
(the Northern Crown)

VIRGO

Zubeneschamali

Zubenelgenubi

LIBRA
(the Scales)

Chow

Unuk al Hay

SERPENS
(the Serpent)

CENTAURUS

LUPUS

☆ M 13
☆ Keystone

Korneforos

☆ M 92

Graffias

Antares ★

SCORPIUS
(the Scorpion)

HERCULES

Ras Algethi

OPHIUCHUS
(the Serpent-Holder)

Shaula

NOVA

Rasalhague

Cebalrai

☆ M 14

M 20 ☆
M 8 ☆

SERPENS

Vega
★ LYRA
Sheliak
☆ M 57
LYRA
(the Harp)

Kaus
Australis

CORONA
AUSTRALIS
(the Southern Crown)

Albireo

Nunki

Arkab

☆ M 27

Tarazed

AQUILA
(the Eagle)

Rukbat

CYGNUS
(the Swan)

variable star

SAGITTARIUS
(the Archer)

Sualocin
Rotanev

Altair
Alshain

Deneb ★

DELPHINUS
(the Dolphin)

AQUARIUS

CAPRICORNUS

ECLIPTIC

but they were put at opposite ends of the heavens so that they would never do battle again. Orion is seen in the winter sky, Scorpius in the summer.

Antares marks the heart of the scorpion and is the fifteenth-brightest star in the sky. The ancient peoples of the Near East also regarded Antares as evil, calling him the Grave Digger of Caravans. But the ancient Chinese looked on the star as one to be worshiped as a safeguard against fire. They named it Huo Shing, meaning "the fire star." Antares has long been thought of as the rival of the red planet Mars. The Greek name for Mars is Ares, and Antares get its name from *Ant-ares,* meaning the "rival of Mars." And so it is. When Mars and Antares are both visible, their red fires rival each other for our attention.

Portrait of Antares

Surface temperature: 3,000 kelvins
Energy output: 9,000 times more than the Sun
Diameter: 400 times larger than the Sun
Mass: 10 or more times that of the Sun
Distance: 520 light-years

When we compare Antares and Mars, we must remember that Mars is but a nearby planet smaller than Earth, while Antares is a distant supergiant star with a diameter 400 times that of the Sun and more than 80,000 times that of Mars. And it pours out 9,000 times more light, heat, and other energy than the Sun does. Antares's distance from us is about 520 light-years. Despite its great size, it has only about ten or fifteen times more mass than the

Sun. That means that, like Betelgeuse, Antares's outer gases are spread out so thinly that the star is a "red-hot vacuum." Also, like Betelgeuse, Antares is a variable star with a period of about five years.

ALDEBARAN AND ARCTURUS

Red giants that can rival Antares and Betelgeuse are few, and Aldebaran is not one of them. Even so, Aldebaran is a fair-sized red giant that shines brightly in the fall and winter evening sky. It marks the fierce red eye of the constellation Taurus, the Bull. Taurus is a winter constellation near Orion (see page 41). To find Aldebaran, just follow the line formed by Orion's three belt stars up and to the right and you will bump into Aldebaran. It is the fourteenth-brightest star in the sky. It has a diameter some 40 times greater than the Sun's and gives off about 125 times more energy than the Sun does. Aldebaran lies at a distance of about 68 light-years.

Portrait of Aldebaran

Surface temperature: 5,000 kelvins
Energy output: 125 times more than the Sun
Diameter: 40 times larger than the Sun
Mass: (not known)
Distance: 68 light-years

Another spectacular star in the giant class is Arcturus, in the constellation Boötes, the Herdsman, visible in spring. It is the fourth-brightest star in the sky and is the brightest-appearing star in the northern sky. It lies at a close distance of only 37 light-years, which makes it one of our nearest neighbors. To find Arcturus, first find the Big Dipper. Then sight away from the four bowl-stars, following the curved handle of the Dipper, and arc down to Arcturus.

Arcturus is about 25 times larger than the Sun in diameter and gives off about 115 times more energy. It has only about four times more mass than the Sun. Because its surface gases are about 4,200 kelvins, a bit hotter than Betelgeuse and Antares, Arcturus shines with a hotter reddish yellow light than the other two stars.

Portrait of Arcturus

Surface temperature: 4,200 kelvins
Energy output: 115 times more than the Sun
Diameter: 25 times larger than the Sun
Mass: (not known)
Distance: 37 light-years

CAPELLA, A HEAD STAR, AND A GARNET STAR

Capella, the brightest star in the constellation Auriga, is the sixth-brightest-appearing star in the sky. It can be seen from the United States on any clear winter night, although it sets below the horizon when viewed from the southern states. To find it, look for the brightest star straight up the sky from Orion. Only 45 light-years away, it appears a golden yellow and shines with the brightness of about 150 Suns.

When we look at Capella we see the combined light of a double

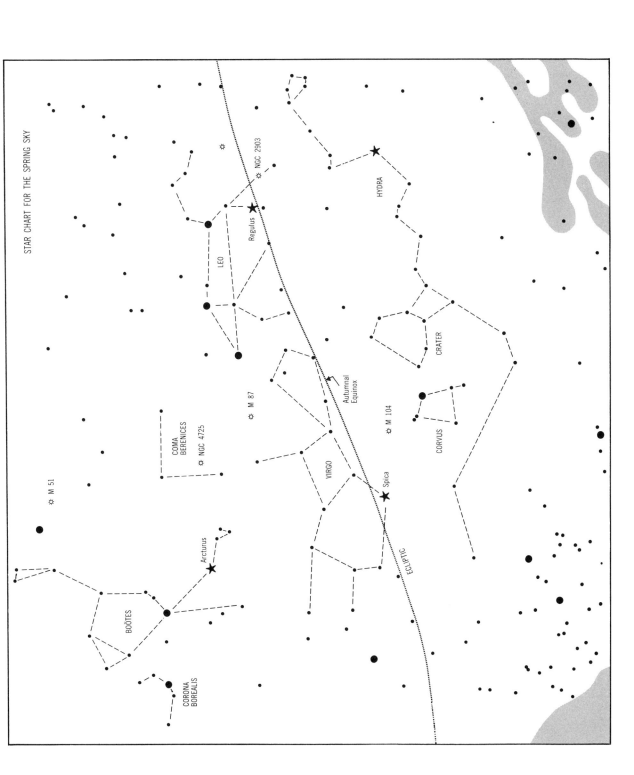

STAR CHART FOR THE SPRING SKY

M 51

CORONA BOREALIS

BOÖTES

Arcturus

COMA BERENICES

NGC 4725

M 87

VIRGO

Spica

ECLIPTIC

Autumnal Equinox

LEO

Regulus

NGC 2903

HYDRA

CRATER

CORVUS

M 104

star. The two stars are about 113 million kilometers (70 million miles) apart, less than the Sun's distance from Earth. The larger of the two, Capella A, is thirteen times larger than the Sun in diameter and three times more massive. Capella A and its companion Capella B are nearly equally bright.

Portrait of Capella

Surface temperature: 5,500 kelvins
Energy output: each star about 75 times more than the Sun
Diameter: 13 times larger than the Sun
Mass: 3 times that of the Sun
Distance: 45 light-years

A roundup of red giants and supergiants would not be complete without mentioning the two superstars Ras Algethi and the Garnet Star. Ras Algethi is the second-brightest star in the faint summer constellation named after the giant of myth, Hercules. Hercules is found just to the right of the constellation Cygnus. *Ras Algethi* means "the kneeler's head" in Arabic, and the star

---

Portrait of Ras Algethi

Surface temperature: 3,000 kelvins
Energy output: 830 times more than the Sun
Diameter: 400 times larger than the Sun
Mass: only a few times that of the Sun
Distance: 430 light-years

---

marks the head of the giant. At a distance of some 400 light-years, it is one of the largest known red giant stars, with a diameter more than 400 times that of the Sun. Except for Betelgeuse and the Garnet Star, Ras Algethi is the largest known star visible to the naked eye.

The Garnet Star is in the constellation Cepheus, the King. It is straight across the northern sky from the Big Dipper and has been described as the reddest star visible. The Garnet Star is another variable star. It outshines even the great Betelgeuse and Deneb, which makes it the most luminous of all known red supergiant stars. It is a distant star, some 1,800 light-years away. Even so, it is an interesting star for amateur astronomers. As it varies from bright to dim and back to bright again, it sometimes appears as a deep orange-red and at other times has a slight purple color.

Portrait of the Garnet Star

Surface temperature: 3,000 kelvins
Energy output: more than 14,000 times that of the Sun
Diameter: several hundred times larger than the Sun
Mass: (not known)
Distance: 1,800 light-years

With this introduction to some of the typical supergiants, you will have a lot to look for as you learn to find your way around the night sky. You should also have a better understanding of the Sun as a star. We will sharpen that understanding even more by comparing the Sun with stars at the opposite end of the size scale—the dwarf stars.

Mighty-Star: The Fascinating Dwarfs

We can think of a star as a huge collection of atoms all being pulled by gravity in toward a common center—the star's core. A star keeps shining as a "normal" star for as long as the hot central furnace in the star's core keeps pushing enough energy up toward the surface to keep the tumbling atoms from falling into the core. That is the secret of star life.

The final stages of a star begin when the nuclear furnace in the core runs down. That happens when the star has used up the last of its hydrogen fuel. This is the most fascinating and dramatic stage in the life of any star. It is the onset of the star's death. Sometimes it happens quietly, other times violently.

THE SUN: FROM RED GIANT TO WHITE DWARF

As you found in the previous chapter, when a star like the Sun uses up the last of its hydrogen fuel, gases in the core region can no longer keep the star puffed up. The cooling core lets the overlying gases tumble inward with a crushing and explosive force. While the temperature of the outer gas layers of the star remains the same, the temperature in the core soars to 200 million kelvins. That is hot enough to cause the store of helium in the core to begin fusing into carbon. This new source of energy then causes the star to puff up and become a red giant, and it remains that way for many thousands of years.

We can imagine the time, some five billion years from now, when the Sun will use up the last of its hydrogen fuel and puff up into red gianthood. As it grows larger, its hot surface gases will swallow up Mercury, the planet closest to the Sun, and vaporize the planet. As it grows still larger, it will next gobble up Venus. Meanwhile, our planet's climate will have grown warmer with the red-giant Sun's approach. The polar ice will melt and cause a rise in sea level of perhaps 90 meters (300 feet). That will be enough to flood whatever coastal cities may exist in that far distant future. Then the oceans will heat up. By this time life in the tropics and as far north as Maine will be unbearable because of the heat. Those animals that survive the warming climate will migrate farther north where it is cooler, for a while at least.

As the Sun continucs to swell as a red giant, Earth will grow hotter and hotter, until life on its surface will be impossible. The oceans will boil and evaporate away. In time, the very rock form-ing Earth's crust will melt and flow. Earth will become a molten dead planet.

Eventually, the Sun will stop swelling. Its nuclear furnace core will be shut down forever. Sunlike stars do not have enough mass to fuse carbon into heavier elements. So once again the Sun will collapse in on itself.

As it does, it will no longer heat Earth, so Earth will begin to cool. The huge stores of water vapor in the atmosphere will condense and fall as rain. The surface rocks will be cooled and once again there will be oceans. But as the Sun continues to shrink,

Earth will grow colder and colder. The centuries-long rains will turn to snow, and the oceans will freeze. It will snow for thousands of years until the last parcel of water vapor is wrung out of the atmosphere. Earth will become locked in a planet-wide ice age that will last forever.

The Sun's final collapse will end in a star 100 times smaller than before, one not much larger than Earth itself. All of its matter will be squeezed into an object so small that it will be denser than anything we can imagine. One teaspoon of that matter will weigh a ton, about the weight of a small car. The Sun will have become a white dwarf star. Its change from a red giant to a white dwarf will have taken perhaps 100,000 years.

Before examining a few white dwarfs visible in the sky now, let's follow the future of our white dwarf Sun. It will continue to shine with an intense white light for a few billion more years. But all the while it will be cooling and dimming. Eventually it will cool so much that it will no longer shine with visible light. When it reaches that stage, it will best be described as a black dwarf, a cold black star with seven frozen planets invisibly circling it until the end of time.

No one has ever seen a black dwarf, but astronomers think that they must be lurking out there in the dark. What other future can there be for a cooling white dwarf? With its nuclear furnace shut down for good, the star has no way to generate new stores of energy. So it must one day burn out and end its life as a cold, dark ball of solid ash.

WHITE DWARFS ON PARADE

Until recently, astronomers knew of only a few hundred white dwarf stars. But today several thousand are known. Because they are such dim objects, radiating so little energy, they must be fairly nearby to be seen at all. Recall from Chapter 5 that Sirius B, the "Pup" companion star of Sirius, is a well-known white dwarf. Like some other white dwarfs, the Pup is about as massive as the Sun. But we know the masses of only a few white dwarfs. Another, known as 40 Eridani B (in the constellation Eridanus, the River), is only about half as massive as the Sun. And a third one, known as Procyon B (the brightest star in the constellation Canis Minor, the Little Dog), is a little more than half as massive as the Sun.

Mass of Three White Dwarfs Compared with Sun

White Dwarf	*Relation to Sun's Mass*
The Pup	about the same
Procyon B	a little more than half
40 Eridani B	about half

All white dwarfs are the size of planets rather than the much larger size of normal stars. The Pup, for example, is only 22,500 kilometers (14,000 miles) in diameter, which is 50 times smaller than the Sun. A star called van Maanen's Star, in the constellation Pisces, the Fishes, probably is a bit smaller than Earth. Among the smallest white dwarf stars known is one in the constellation Draco, the Dragon. It is half the size of Earth. A still smaller one, in the constellation Taurus, the Bull, seems to be only 1,900 kilometers (1,200 miles) in diameter. That is about half the Moon's size. The smallest white dwarf discovered so far is in the constellation Cetus, the Whale, and may have a diameter of only 1,600 kilometers (1,000 miles). One astronomer has said we should call such unusually small dwarfs "pigmy" stars.

Size of Five White Dwarfs

White Dwarf	Diameter (in miles)
The Pup	14,000
van Maanen's Star	7,000(?)
Dwarf in Draco	4,000
Dwarf in Taurus	1,200
Dwarf in Cetus	1,000(?)

Recall how dim the white dwarfs are? For example, the Pup is 435 times less bright than the Sun. One of the dimmest white dwarfs known (in the constellation Virgo, the Virgin) is 15,000 times fainter than the Sun. One of the dimmest of all white dwarfs is one in the constellation Volans, the Flying Fish. It is 35,000 times fainter than the Sun. At the opposite extreme, one of the brightest white dwarfs known (in the constellation Canes Venatici, the Hunting Dogs) is only 40 times less bright than the Sun.

Most of the white dwarfs have very high surface temperatures. They must have, since they shine with an intense white light. But again, these stars are so small and so distant that they appear dim. More than half are from 8,000 to 10,000 kelvins (recall that the Sun's surface gases are 6,000 kelvins). A few are even hotter and shine with a bluish white light. The cooling time for white dwarfs is very long. It may take about three billion years for a blue-white hot dwarf to cool to a yellowish white dwarf. Van Maanen's Star may have been a white dwarf for the past five billion or so years.

Perhaps the most interesting thing about the white dwarfs is their densities, or how tightly packed their matter is. You know that a bowling ball weighs more than a ball of cotton the same

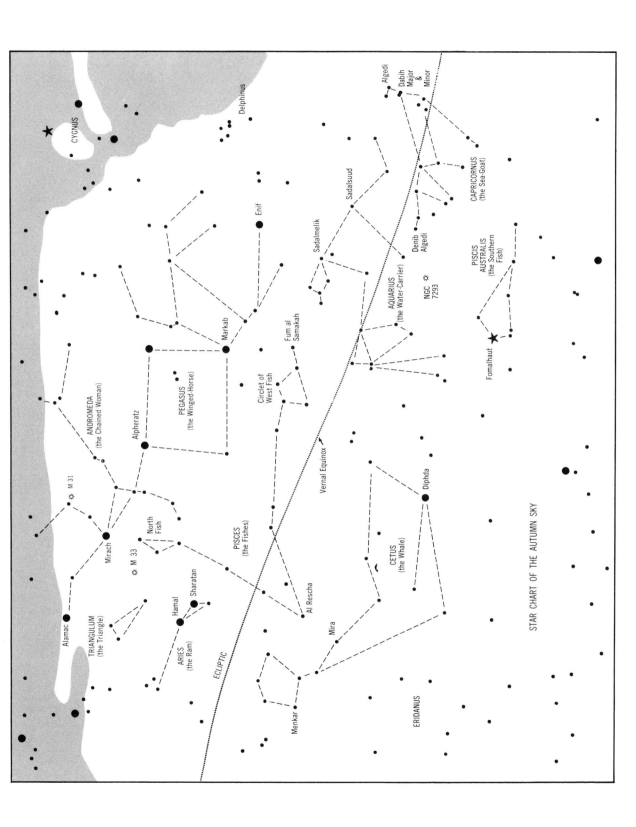

CYGNUS

Delphinus

Algedi
Dabih
Major
&
Minor

CAPRICORNUS
(the Sea-Goat)

Sadalsuud

Enif

Sadalmelik

Denib
Algedi

NGC ☆
7293

PISCIS
AUSTRALIS
(the Southern
Fish)

AQUARIUS
(the Water-Carrier)

Fum al
Samakah

Markab

Circlet of
West Fish

Fomalhaut

ANDROMEDA
(the Chained Woman)

Alpheratz

PEGASUS
(the Winged-Horse)

Vernal Equinox

☆ M 31

Mirach

North
Fish

Diphda

☆ M 33

PISCES
(the Fishes)

CETUS
(the Whale)

Alamac

Sharatan

Hamal

Al Rescha

TRIANGULUM
(the Triangle)

ARIES
(the Ram)

Mira

STAR CHART OF THE AUTUMN SKY

ECLIPTIC

Menkar

ERIDANUS

size. That is because the bowling ball has more mass, or matter, packed into the same amount of space. In other words, the bowling ball is denser than the ball of cotton.

Now think of an atom with its dense center of tightly packed protons and neutrons, and with its electrons whizzing around the center. Lots of space is taken up by those darting electrons, so in a way a whole atom complete with electrons is something like our ball of cotton. The atom isn't very tightly packed. But when atoms are broken apart, as they are inside stars, their individual electrons, protons, and neutrons get mashed tightly together. That is the crowded state of affairs inside a white dwarf star.

Remember the questions asked back on page 51? A teaspoon of tightly packed matter from the Pup would weigh about two and a half tons! But as white dwarfs go, the Pup is not especially dense. Van Maanen's Star weighs about 20 tons a teaspoonful. The white dwarf known as Wolf 219 is smaller than Earth and weighs about 100 tons a teaspoonful. The record holder may be the star listed as LP 768-500. It has a diameter of only a few hundred miles but weighs about 18,000 tons a teaspoonful! By comparison, the Sun weighs only half an ounce a teaspoonful.

White dwarfs may exist as single stars, or as one member of a double-star pair, or as both members. Paired white dwarfs seem to be rare, however. Only three are known, although there are a few other good candidates. One star catalog lists a total of 320 double-star systems containing white dwarfs. Sirius and Procyon are examples of double stars with one white dwarf companion.

NOVA STARS

Stars called novae explode and grow much brighter over a period of days or weeks, then return to normal again, usually over several years. Although we have ideas about nova stars, we have a lot more to learn about them. About 100 novae have been seen and reported throughout history, but astronomers think that more than a dozen unseen ones may flare up in our galaxy every year. Could there be a connection between novae and white dwarfs? Maybe. When a red giant collapses and is well on its way to white dwarfhood, it may go through one or more periods of being unstable. At such times the star may erupt as a nova. This may be especially so of the more massive stars.

Most novae may be one star in a double-star pair. The star about to become a nova is the denser of the two—a white dwarf or a star becoming one. The denser star pulls matter away from its less dense companion by gravitation. The matter, mostly hydrogen, collects at the denser star's surface. Eventually the bottom of this collected layer of hydrogen heats up enough to explode. When that happens, the star blasts away the outer layer of matter, in the process becoming a nova. Such flare-ups may occur more than once for a white dwarf with a close companion. Single stars that flare up as novae must collect and build up their outer layer of hydrogen from nearby clouds of gas and dust since they do not have companion stars. The nova known as the star WZ, in the constellation Sagitta, the Arrow, has been seen to explode three times, once in 1913, again in 1946, and most recently in 1978. Most likely it has exploded more than three times. There are more of these so-called recurrent novae.

The matter cast off by one of these exploding stars forms a great gas bubble, or shell, around the star. At such times a recurrent nova is called a shell star. The one shown here is in the constellation Aquarius, the Water Bearer. In the photograph, the shell appears as a flat ring around the central star rather than as a three-dimensional shell. That is because we are looking through a greater thickness of the shell's gas out around the edge of the gas bubble than if we looked through the bubble directly at the

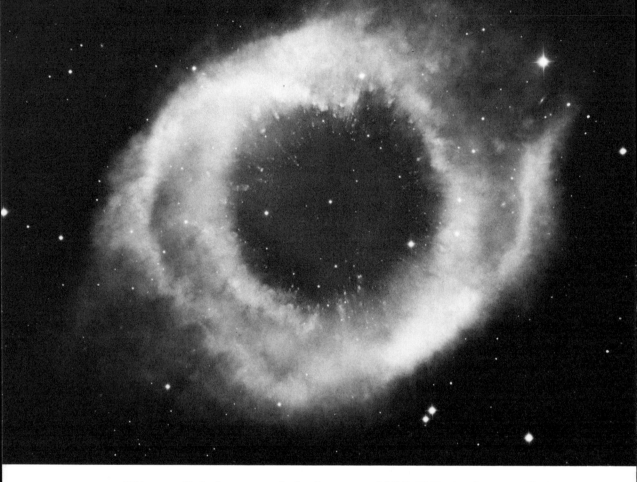

This so-called planetary nebula, known as NGC 7293, in the constellation Aquarius is an example of a shell star. Palomar Observatory

central star. This particular shell of gas is expanding at the rate of about sixteen kilometers (ten miles) a second.

One of the brightest nova stars known exploded into view on the evening of August 27, 1975. It occurred in the constellation Cygnus, the Swan, and was named Nova Cygni. What was a distant and dim star about 4,000 light-years away brightened in only a few days to 40 million times its normal brightness! That made it equal in brightness to 500,000 Suns. Just before peak brightness, the shell of gas cast off by the explosion was cast outward at a speed of 1,930 kilometers (1,200 miles) a second. That speed is typical of other bright novae. About four months after the flare-up, the star returned to normal.

On the night of June 8, 1918, a star in the constellation Aquila, the Eagle, flared up as a nova. On exploding, it blasted off several gas shells. In only a few hours it became the brightest star, except for Sirius, in the northern sky. Before, the star had been too dim to be seen without a telescope. By the end of the month Nova Aquilae, as it was named, was barely visible again. Today the star is a hot, bluish dwarf star smaller than the Sun.

Nova Herculis, in the constellation Hercules, burst into view as a blazing star just before Christmas 1934. It was one of the brightest novae of this century. Before the explosion, the star had

---

Nova stars are stars that suddenly increase in brightness and then return to normal. Shown here is Nova Herculis, seen as it normally appears (*left*), and then as it appeared on March 10, 1935, when it flared up as a nova. Lick Observatory

been a very dim object visible only through a telescope, at a distance of some 1,200 light-years. At its brightest it outshone the Sun by 65,000 times. The star remained bright for about 100 nights before fading again to a dim object. Because of its lingering nature, Nova Herculis is termed a "slow nova." Like Nova Aquilae, Nova Herculis is now a hot, bluish dwarf star.

Twenty years after it exploded, astronomers found Nova Herculis to be a binary star with one component periodically eclipsing the other, as with Epsilon Aurigae. But it had a period of only 4 hours and 39 minutes instead of 27 years. That is one of the shortest-period eclipsing double stars known. The two stars are very close, a bit closer than Earth and the Moon.

PLANETARY NEBULAE

If you have a small telescope, you will be able to search the constellation Lyra, the Harp, and find the famous Ring Nebula. But it will take a 6-inch telescope to see the tiny ghostly doughnut of gas floating in space and surrounding a central star. The star with its gas cloud is too dim to be seen with the naked eye. Stars like this one were named "planetary nebulae" in the 1700s because they were mistaken for planets within the Solar System. Their faint greenish color gives them the appearance of the planet Uranus. There may be about 10,000 planetary nebulae in our galaxy, and two or so new ones may form each year.

The bright central star within the Ring Nebula is a bluish dwarf that appears to be on its way to becoming a white dwarf. It has a surface temperature of about 100,000 kelvins, which seems to be typical of such stars. They are among the hottest stars known. The Ring Nebula is about 1,500 light-years away.

Astronomers have yet to find out what makes the star at its center cast off gases into space. Maybe such stars have just gone

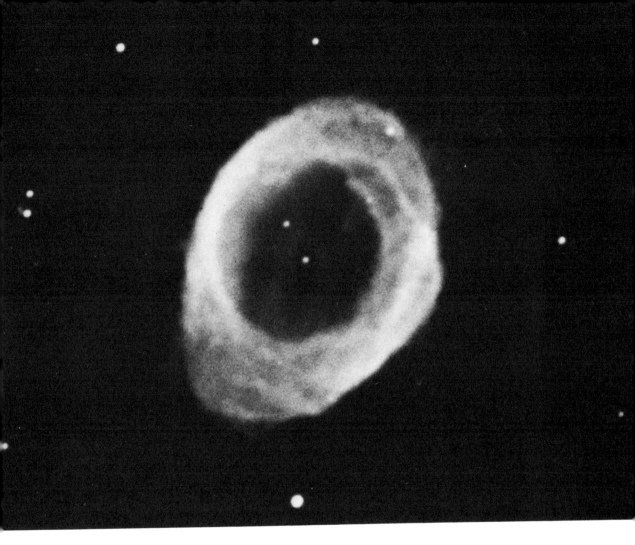

The planetary nebulae also are emission nebulae. The Ring Nebula in the constellation Lyra shown here is typical of these roughly sphere-shaped gas clouds. Palomar Observatory

through the red-giant stage and are shrinking rapidly. As they do, they leave some of their outer gas layers behind. The gas then expands off into space as a planetary nebula cloud. But this happens much more slowly than the gas cloud hurled off by an exploding nova.

RED DWARFS

Recall that the red dwarfs are small stars with not very much mass, less than the Sun has. They have surface temperatures of about 3,000 kelvins or less. The core temperatures of some are about 10 million kelvins, just hot enough to turn on the nuclear furnace and fuse hydrogen into helium in the core region. So those red dwarfs are shining by fusion reactions, which is not the case with white dwarfs. Red dwarfs are stars in midlife, while white dwarfs are the remains of burned-out stars.

Some red dwarfs, however, have core temperatures too low to fuse hydrogen. Then are they technically "stars"? We will have more to say about these interesting objects at the end of the chapter, when we talk about "brown dwarfs." In general, the small amount of mass making up red dwarfs makes them feeble radiators of energy. Because they are such weak energy producers, they have the longest life spans of all stars. They may shine on for a trillion years.

One of the most famous red dwarfs is found in the constellation Aquila, the Eagle, and goes by the name of van Biesbroeck's Star. It is one of the least luminous stars known and was not spotted until the year 1943. It turned out to be a nearby double star about 20 light-years away. The larger star of the pair is the one first sighted and is so feeble that it would take 250 more stars like it to equal the Sun.

Some 20 years ago Edward Upton wrote the following about van Biesbroeck's Star:

> Van Biesbroeck's Star is so faint
> It's either a star or it ain't.
> There has even been talk
> That it's only a rock
> Covered with luminous paint.

Van Biesbroeck's Star probably has a core too cool to fuse hydrogen and may well be on its way to cooling and dimming as a black dwarf object. There must be many such "stars" out there, but they shine so feebly that we cannot see them, even with powerful telescopes.

Another well-known red dwarf is Alpha Centauri. Located in the constellation Centaurus, the Centaur, it is our closest neighboring star beyond the Solar System, only 4.3 light-years away, or about 25 trillion miles. It has a red dwarf companion called Proxima Centauri, among the dimmest stars known. It would take 13,000 stars like it to equal the energy output of the Sun. The diameter of this red dwarf star is only 64,400 kilometers (40,000 miles), about half the size of Jupiter.

FLARE STARS

Although tiny as stars go, Proxima Centauri is an interesting star. It belongs to that class of stars called flare stars. For some reason we do not understand very well, these stars send out flashes of light and then dim rapidly. The star may be back to normal within a half-hour or so. Proxima Centauri flared up at least 48 times between 1925 and 1950. The flares on Proxima Centauri have been described as "local hot spots." On the Sun, where they are common, they are called "solar flares." But the Sun's flares are not widespread enough to cause the Sun to become visibly brighter overall. It is quite likely that most stars have local hot spots but are too bright for their flares to show. We can see them on the Sun because of the Sun's closeness, and we can see them on red dwarfs because the surfaces of those stars are so dim that a sudden bright patch stands out.

The most violent red dwarf flare star known is the one in the constellation Cetus, the Whale. It is called UV Ceti. It is a double star, and the two companions are among the smallest and least massive stars known. The Sun has 800 times more mass than both companions of UV Ceti combined. The smaller of the two is the more interesting, and is the flare star. Its outbursts are sudden and over within two or three minutes. In 1952 the star flared up and increased its brightness by 75 times in only 20 seconds. More recently, in October 1963, astronomers recorded fourteen flares on UV Ceti in 82 hours.

BROWN DWARFS

Since planets and stars form out of the same cosmic soup of gas and dust under gravity, what is the difference between them? In one word, the answer is mass. If the object has enough mass so that the core temperature is pushed high enough to ignite a nuclear fire, then the object becomes a star. If it does not have enough mass to raise the core temperature that high, the object becomes a lone nonstar object in space. Or if it is a member of a planetary system, it becomes a planet.

The planet Jupiter is an example of just such a "near-miss" object. Jupiter gives off more energy than it receives from the Sun—twice as much. Could Jupiter have been much hotter in its early history, maybe hot enough to have warmed its four large moons as the Sun warms the inner planets today?

It seems so. Imagine the scene 4.6 billion years ago, when the Solar System was taking shape. Jupiter, two and a half times as massive as all the other planets combined, began as an enormous gas ball that contracted and heated up, just as the infant Sun was doing. But, unlike the Sun, Jupiter lacked enough mass to send its core temperature high enough to ignite a nuclear fire. The core reached only a few tens of thousands of degrees. So Jupiter became only hot enough to glow cherry red, like a red dwarf star. For a while it bathed its inner moons in light and heat, but that energy faded as the planet slowly cooled. Its fate as a planet was sealed. To have become a star, Jupiter would have needed 80 times more mass than it now has. Although that is about 800 times less mass than the Sun has, it would have been mass enough to have made Jupiter a dim red dwarf star. In that case, the Sun would have become a double star.

What of objects midway between Jupiter and the smallest true stars? The first such object was discovered in December 1984, in the constellation Ophiuchus, the Serpent Bearer, and was given the name van Biesbroeck 8B, a companion of van Biesbroeck's Star, mentioned earlier. Its mass is only several dozen times more than Jupiter's. With a surface temperature of only 1,400 kelvins, it is only hot enough to glow like an ember. Astronomers have decided to call this new class of nonstar objects brown dwarfs. Brown dwarfs may exist throughout the galaxy by the millions. They may exist singly or as companions of double- or triple-star systems. But most are so far away, and so dim, that detecting them is very hard. Van Biesbroeck 8B was found because of its closeness of about 20 light-years.

Several of the stars described so far are not steady shiners. Instead, they flare up brightly at times and then return to their normal dim state. Such stars belong to a class of fascinating stars called variable stars, which we will look at next.

Stars Who Can't Make Up Their Minds: Variables

Many stars go through cycles of bright to dim as if they can't make up their minds how to shine. At least one observer has said this might simply be a way of calling attention to themselves. They are called variable stars. More than 25,000 have been listed, but most stars may become variables at some stage in their lives. We can arrange them into two main groups. In one group are the explosive variables like shell stars, which cast off enormous shells of gas; nova stars, which swell up from time to time and become many times brighter than usual; and supernova stars, which end their lives in catastrophic explosions. We will have a look at supernova stars in the next chapter. In this chapter we will examine the second class of variable stars, the group called pulsating variables.

MIRA-TYPE VARIABLES

Most of the known pulsating variable stars are of the Mira type, named after the first such star discovered, in the year 1596. When at its brightest, Mira, meaning "the wonderful," in Latin, can be easily seen as a reddish star in the constellation Cetus, the Whale.

About 4,000 Mira variables are listed in star catalogs. However, you need a telescope to see most of them.

All Mira variables are red giant stars with surface temperatures ranging from about 1,900 to 2,600 kelvins. At those temperatures, a star's surface gases glow with a deep reddish light. The typical period, or time of completing one cycle of going from dim to bright and back to dim again, is 300 days for a Mira variable. During a period a Mira variable becomes about fifteen times brighter than when dimmest.

Mira itself is one of the ten largest stars we can see. It has a diameter about 400 times greater than the Sun's. But when fully swollen, Mira may grow to 500 times the Sun's diameter. Despite its great size, the star is another red-hot vacuum. Mira is a double star with a blue dwarf companion about 3,300 times denser than the Sun. Mira's period averages 331 days, but the star typically does not stick to a rigid schedule.

Another prominent Mira-type variable is found in Cygnus, the Swan, and is known as Chi Cygni. When at its brightest, it is seen to stand out from the surrounding stars like a glowing red beacon, shining with a stronger red light than Mira itself. Chi Cygni's period averages 407 days. At brightest it may be 10,000 times brighter than when dimmest, but the average increase is about 3,000 times. The star is a true red giant, about the size of Mira and with a low surface temperature of about 1,900 kelvins. Its distance is uncertain. It may be from 200 to 400 light-years away.

What makes the Mira-type variables swell up and shrink in fairly predictable periods is still pretty much of a mystery. One theory is that these red giant stars are in advanced old age. They may have reached the stage when their hydrogen fuel supply has nearly run out and the fusion of hydrogen into helium has slowed. The stars may have begun to switch over to fusing helium into

This globular cluster of stars seen in the constellation Hercules is typical of other such clusters forming a halo around the nucleus of the Milky Way. The globular clusters contain many old and aging stars. Palomar Observatory

carbon as a source of energy production. The switchover may account for the variations in their energy output.

RR LYRAE VARIABLES

Another large class of pulsating variable stars is the RR Lyrae variables, named after the first such variable star discovered, in the year 1901. That star is seen in the summer sky constellation Lyra, the Harp (see page 55). The RR Lyrae variables all are white or yellow-white giants, but none is visible without a telescope. We know of more than 3,000 of them in the Milky Way galaxy.

The pulselike brightening of these stars is much shorter than that of Mira-type variables. They also stick to a much tighter schedule of pulsing. Most take from six to eighteen hours to complete one period. They are quick to brighten, but somewhat slower to dim back to normal again. A typical variable may double in brightness in less than half an hour, then fade back to dim in about four hours. All the RR Lyrae variables pour out just about the same amount of energy. All are from 50 to 65 times brighter than the Sun, and are six to seven times the Sun's diameter.

The RR Lyrae variables are sprinkled throughout our galaxy. Some are members of those distant clusters of stars called globular clusters. The globular clusters form a spherical halo around the central region of our galaxy. Each cluster contains from hundreds of thousands to millions of stars arranged in a great ball.

Because the RR Lyrae variable stars all shine with just about the same energy output, astronomers can use them as cosmic yardsticks to measure distances within our home galaxy. Measuring the distance to an RR Lyrae variable in any one of the globular clusters gives us the distance to the cluster. And measuring the distance of the RR Lyrae stars at the farthest reaches of our galaxy tells us how large the galaxy is. It turns out to be 100,000 light-years from edge to edge. The Sun is about 30,000 light-years from the galactic center, or nucleus.

BEACONS OF THE UNIVERSE: THE CEPHEIDS

The best-known, but not the most numerous, pulsating variables are the Cepheid variables. They are named after the first such star observed in 1784, Delta Cephei, in the northern sky constellation Cepheus, the King.

All the Cepheids are hot white and yellow giants with tightly scheduled periods that can often be measured down to a fraction of a second. Their periods range from a few hours up to about 50 days, but most are from five to eight days. These stars may be a stage in star life between the young blue giant stars and the much older red giants.

Delta Cephei itself has a period of 5 days, 8 hours, and 48 minutes. It is a yellowish white supergiant on the average between 25 and 30 times larger than the Sun. When brightest, it is some 3,300 times the Sun's brightness. The star is about 1,000 light-years away.

The Cepheid variables also can be used as cosmic yardsticks. Unlike the RR Lyrae variables, the Cepheid variables are bright enough to be seen in galaxies beyond our own. The world's largest telescopes reveal billions upon billions of galaxies seemingly stretching across the universe without end. Astronomers knew of those other galaxies long before they were able to measure their distances from us. Then in the year 1924, Edwin Hubble used Cepheid variables as a yardstick to measure the distance to the beautiful Andromeda Galaxy (see page 30). He could see

There appears to be no end to the galaxies that can be photographed through the world's largest telescopes. Many galaxies, of many shapes, are seen in this splendid cluster of galaxies visible in the constellation Hercules. In the bowl region of the Big Dipper, telescopes reveal about half a million galaxies.

Mount Wilson and Las Campanas Observatories, Carnegie Institution of Washington

Cepheid variables in Andromeda and so was able to estimate that galaxy's distance of some 2 million light-years.

ERUPTIVE VARIABLES

Variable stars sometimes come in surprising packages. There is a class of variables called eruptive variables because they do just that, erupt from time to time. One such star is in the constellation Cygnus, the Swan, and is called SS Cygni. In fact, all the stars in this class are called SS Cygni stars. They are bluish dwarfs, sort of mininovae that erupt several times a year. But the eruptions do not even come close to matching a nova outburst. During a typical eruption the star may become 100 times brighter than normal. After staying bright for a few days, it then slowly fades to dim again.

Like most nova stars, the eruptive variables also seem to be members of double-star systems in which the two stars are fairly close together and revolve about each other fairly rapidly. And it may be that the eruptive star in a pair is the more massive and denser of the two stars. Because it is, it pulls away surface gases from the other star in the pair. Those gases then fuel the eruptions of the eruptive variable star. The longer it takes such a star to build up matter for an eruption, the more violent the eruption seems to be. Astronomers wonder if the SS Cyngi stars eventually turn into full-scale nova stars. Or perhaps it is the other way around—that nova stars eventually settle down as the less violent eruptive stars. The puzzle remains to be solved.

FLASH STARS

The Pleiades star cluster in the constellation Taurus, the Bull, has several rather interesting faint red dwarfs that are variable stars.

The stars flash into brightness and may remain bright from a few minutes up to three hours. Altogether, about half a dozen such stars are known; they are called flash stars. Some astronomers think that flash stars may be new stars in the process of heating up but not yet hot enough for their nuclear furnaces to ignite.

THE ODD COUPLE

Probably the most unusual variable star in the sky is one named Beta Lyrae, in the constellation Lyra, the Harp. Its popular name is Sheliak, from the Arabic *Al Shilyak,* meaning "the tortoise." It is a double star, an eclipsing binary like Epsilon Aurigae. But Beta Lyrae is a special case that has caught the attention of and mystified astronomers ever since the star was first described in 1784.

You can watch the star without a telescope, but studying it through binoculars or a small telescope is better. The period of dimming and brightening is very nearly thirteen days. The dimming occurs each time one member of the pair circles around behind the other member and so is blocked from view. Whenever the two stars are side by side in their orbits about each other, they appear at their brightest. The major star of the pair is a giant about nineteen times larger and 3,000 times brighter than the Sun. The companion star seems to be about fifteen times larger than the Sun, which makes the pair one of the largest double-star systems known.

The fascinating thing about the pair is the result of their closeness. They are only 35 million kilometers (22 million miles) apart. That is about Earth's distance from the planet Venus, and it is exceptionally close for star pairs. Because they are so close, and so massive, a gravitational tug-of-war goes on between the two stars all the time.

As each star pulls on the other, each is stretched out a bit into the shape of an egg rather than the shape of a ball. Gravity also causes the more massive star of the pair to pull surface gases away from the other star. Adding to this gravitational display, gases are cast off by both stars in the form of a huge stream of matter that spirals outward around the two stars. So both stars are steadily losing matter to space. What this will mean in the stars' future is hard to say. Beta Lyrae probably has been studied more than any other distant star, but this odd couple continues to pose a mystery.

T TAURI STARS

Before ending our description of variable stars, we should take a quick look at the star that forms the point of the V marking the face of Taurus, the Bull. It is called T Tauri and is only one of many known stars of its type. These stars are always found in or at the edges of clouds of gas and dust. Many have been discovered within the dark clouds of the Milky Way. They are dwarf variable stars and are somewhat like the Sun in brightness and size. But what makes them very different from the Sun is their unpredictable outbursts that cause them to grow rapidly four or five times brighter than usual.

Astronomers suspect that the T Tauri stars are young. They may be at an age between the flash stars and the Sun. They have not yet settled down to a steady burning, although their nuclear furnaces have been ignited by high core temperatures. These stars may still be growing by attracting matter from the gas and dust clouds associated with them.

It is now time that we turn our attention to the kings of the heavens, the supernova stars, and the fascinating objects—black holes—that they may turn into.

Supernovae, Black Holes, and Goblins

THE CRAB SUPERNOVA

Just to the upper right of the star marking the lower horn tip of Taurus, the Bull, is a faint fuzzy patch that is easily seen through a small telescope. It was discovered in 1731 and has become one of the most studied nebulae in the sky. It is the famous Crab Nebula, the remains of a hot superstar that exploded and blew off its outer gas layers. All that was left of the star was its extremely hot exposed core.

Such stars that explode catastrophically are called supernova stars, and their explosions are the most violent events we have ever seen in the universe, probably the most violent events since the Big Bang with which the universe began. The explosion of the Crab supernova was recorded by Chinese astronomers. Their records of the event indicate that the star exploded on July 4 in the year 1054. According to one Chinese report, the "guest star," as they called it, ". . . was visible in the day like Venus, with pointed rays in all four directions. The color was reddish white. . . . It was seen altogether for twenty-three days [as a daytime object]."

The explosion also may have been observed by at least two American Indian groups. Drawings of what seem to be the supernova have been found in northern Arizona on a wall of Navajo Canyon and in a cave at White Mesa. The clue that the drawn object may be the Crab supernova is its position beside a crescent moon, which was visible when that explosion was observed.

The Crab Nebula in the constellation Taurus is an expanding cloud of gas, the supernova remains of a star observed by Chinese astronomers in the year 1054. Palomar Observatory

Because of the Chinese records, we have a pretty good idea of what people watching the event in 1054 saw. When the star flared up, it shone with the light of 400 million Suns for a few weeks. At a distance of some 6,300 light-years, the star explosion sent a cloud of gas speeding outward at about 1,600 kilometers (1,000 miles) a second. That is one of the highest speeds known in our galaxy. The cloud today—the Crab Nebula—is nearly ten light-years in diameter and still spreading outward.

Only three other supernova explosions are known in our galaxy: One burst into view in the year 1006 in the constellation Lupus, the Wolf, but we know very little about it. Another was the supernova of 1572 in the constellation Cassiopeia, the Queen. It is known as Tycho's Star. The Danish astronomer Tycho Brahe spotted it high overhead on the night of November 11 and saw it outshine Jupiter and then equal Venus in apparent brightness. Tycho described it as ". . . a miracle indeed, one that has never been previously seen before our time, in any age since the beginning of the world." Of course he was wrong. The third supernova seen in our galaxy is known as Kepler's Star. It was first observed on October 9, 1604, in the constellation Ophiuchus, the Serpent Bearer, and was then as bright as Mars. Within a few days it became brighter than Jupiter and stayed that way for several weeks. After eighteen months, the star vanished from view, in March 1606.

Supernova explosions seem to be rare events, at least in our galaxy. But with the world's giant telescopes we see them taking place in galaxies far beyond our own. They sometimes are so bright that they outshine the combined brightness of the billions of other stars in a distant galaxy. In 1885 a supernova explosion in the Andromeda Galaxy puffed up in brightness to equal more than one and a half billion Suns. In August 1937 a supernova exploded in the galaxy listed as IC 4182, becoming 100 times

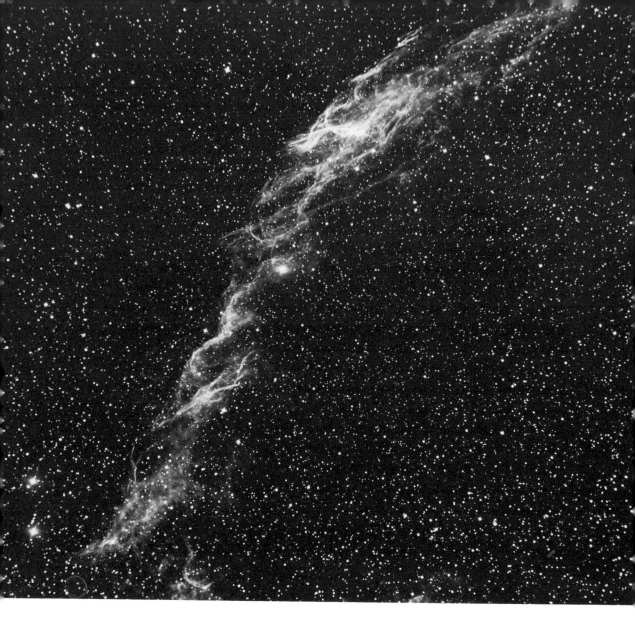

With telescopes and long time exposures, astronomers can photograph graceful veils of gas, the remains of matter hurled off by those catastrophically explosive stars called supernovae. The material hurled off by such stars contains elements heavier than iron. It now seems that a cloud of such matter from a supernova enriched the gas cloud of hydrogen and helium out of which the Sun and planets of the Solar System formed. The supernova matter shown here is invisible in the constellation Cygnus, the Swan.   Mount Wilson and Las Campanas Observatories, Carnegie Institution of Washington brighter than the galaxy itself. In all, more than 100 supernovae have been recorded in our and other galaxies.

Astronomers assign supernovae to one of two classes. Type I explosions are the rarer and brighter, and are equal to about 200 million Suns. They explode into brightness over several days and maintain their brightness for several days more. Then they dim, over a period of about a month.

Type II supernovae outnumber Type I by about ten to one. Type II supernova explosions are not quite so violent as those of Type I, and the Type II stars seem to be younger. Supernovae of this group rapidly build in brightness and remain bright for several days. They dim a bit over about 25 days, then stay some-what bright for between 50 to 100 days. After that they dim rapidly.

NEUTRON STARS

Supernovae are not produced by ordinary stars. These explosions come from the blue-white giants, the superstars described in Chapter 5. These are extremely massive stars, about 30 times more massive than the Sun. A blue-white supergiant keeps fusing hydrogen into helium until its core region has used up most of the hydrogen and is mostly helium. As the hydrogen fusions slow down, the core cools a bit and shrinks. This lets the overlying gases collapse inward, and the core is squeezed in the vise of gravity with a crushing force. The core temperatures become high enough for helium to fuse and form carbon and oxygen. Temperatures keep rising until the fusion of carbon and oxygen produces the heavier element silicon. And finally, the fusions of silicon produce a star with a core of mostly iron, along with some nickel. The star, as a normal shining star, cannot produce elements heavier than iron. It has reached the critical stage of its life.

So the picture we have of this superstar about to become a supernova is something like this: A core of nearly pure iron is burning at one billion kelvins. Enclosing the iron core is a hot shell of silicon fusing into iron. The shell of silicon is surrounded by a shell of carbon and oxygen fusing into silicon. The shell of carbon and oxygen is surrounded by a shell of helium fusing into carbon and oxygen. And finally, the shell of helium is surrounded by a shell of hydrogen fusing into helium. But with its iron core, the star has become unstable.

Eventually, the hydrogen fuel shell is used up, so no more helium can be made to fuel the production of carbon deeper down within the star, and so on. In time, iron production in the core shuts down. The core then begins to cool and is squeezed tighter and tighter by the overlying gases.

The pressure in the core is now so high that something fascinating happens to the iron there. It is crushed to bits. Its neutrons, protons, and other atomic particles are freed. Protons and electrons join and become new neutrons. The star's core becomes a ball of neutrons.

Now, neutrons are different from protons and electrons in a very important way. A ball of protons cannot be packed very tightly together, because all the protons have a positive electrical charge and push away from each other. It is something like the two plus-ends of a bar magnet pushing away from each other when you try to make them touch. No matter how tightly you tried to crush a ball of protons, you would not get very far because of the electrical forces keeping each proton at its distance from all neighboring protons. The same would be true of a ball of electrons, which also have electrical forces preventing them from being closely packed together. But the situation is different for neutrons. Neutrons do not have an electrical charge at all. That means a ball of them can be packed very tightly. So the instant

From time to time we can see supernova explosions in distant galaxies. These two photographs show a galaxy (NGC 4725) in the constellation Coma Berenices. The top photo was taken on May 10, 1940. The bottom photo was taken on January 2, 1941, when a supernova explosion was seen. Mount Wilson and Las Campanas Observatories, Carnegie Institution of Washington

all of the matter in the core of a supernova star is changed from iron into neutrons, the core collapses in on itself under the great weight of all the overlying matter of the star.

In a flash, the gases above the core come falling inward. Neutrons of the outer core region, along with all the overlying gases, are splashed outward in the tremendous explosion that is over in a tiny fraction of a second, and that we call a supernova. During that explosion, so much energy is produced that all the elements heavier than iron—for example, gold, silver, lead, uranium, and so on—are produced and hurled outward as part of the supernova cloud. Over a few months a new supernova may give off as much light as the Sun produces in a billion years.

What is left behind is the exposed and tightly packed inner core of neutrons only about ten kilometers (six miles) in diameter. We call that tiny ball of intensely hot neutrons a neutron star. Its temperature is in the billions of kelvins and its matter is so tightly packed that a teaspoon of it weighs a billion tons! By comparison, a white dwarf seems like a ball of cotton.

PULSARS

The final collapse that produces a neutron star leaves the ball of neutrons spinning very fast. A rapidly spinning neutron star is called a pulsar. Astronomers first detected pulsars in 1967. Today we know of 400 or so of these stars, six of which are members of a double-star system. Some send out two beams of energy that spin around with the star as two hot spots, one at each pole of the pulsar, like the rotating beacon of a lighthouse. Each time the beams of energy sweep around and are caught in the giant dish of a radio telescope, the telescope receives a pulse of radio energy, hence the term "pulsar." The bright object in the center of the Crab Nebula is a pulsar, and the fastest-spinning one known. It is spinning about 30 times a second. But it is slowing down, as all pulsars do.

Something interesting happens to a spinning neutron star as it slows down. First of all, a neutron star's matter is so dense that the star has a solid crust thousands of times tougher than steel. Because the star is spinning, it bulges out a bit at the equator. (Earth's rotation also causes Earth to bulge out a bit at the equator. The distance through our planet at its equator is about 40 kilometers—25 miles—more than the distance through its poles.) As a rotating neutron star slows down, the force that causes it to bulge at the equator weakens. Each time that force weakens enough, the crust around the equator collapses inward an inch or so due to gravity pulling all parts of the crust in toward the core. At such moments of minicollapse there is a starquake. So each starquake tends to make the neutron star a bit more spherical.

Can just about any star become a neutron star? No. It now seems that a star with less than one and a quarter times the mass of the Sun will end its life by shrinking to a white dwarf. Only those stars with more than that amount of mass become supernovae that may end up as neutron stars. What about neutron stars that are still more massive? Neutron stars seem to have an upper limit of mass—a little more than three times more mass than the Sun. If a neutron star passes that mass limit, it becomes what astronomers call a black hole.

BLACK HOLES

One astronomer has described a black hole as an object that dug a hole, jumped in, and then pulled the hole in after itself! Some astronomers question whether these mystery objects even exist.

Those who do believe in black holes describe them this way: When a large burned-out star, say, one that is ten times more massive than the Sun, shrinks to about 60 kilometers (37 miles) in diameter, it becomes very special. It is so dense, and its gravity so strong, that nothing can escape from it, not even light.

That means that we will never be able to "see" a black hole. At this great density the star disappears inside itself, so to speak. If we could squeeze the Sun down into a ball of matter only five and a half kilometers (three and a half miles) in diameter, it would become a black hole. (Because of the smaller mass than that of the star mentioned above, the Sun would have to be crushed into a smaller ball of matter.) After a dying star contracts into a black hole, it continues to contract until it is a point called a singularity.

If energy cannot escape from a black hole, how do astronomers detect one? Suppose that a black hole has a nearby companion star. The strong gravitation of the black hole would pull away a steady stream of the neighboring star's surface gases. The gases are pulled away so violently that they are heated to about a billion kelvins. That is hot enough for the gases to give off bursts of X-ray energy just before the gaseous matter disappears into the black hole. Such X-ray bursts seem to be evidence of the existence of black holes.

To date, the double star known as Cygnus X-1 is the most promising candidate for a black hole. It gives off streams of X rays as its surface gases are being pulled away by a superdense unseen companion that may have fifteen or so times more mass than the Sun—a black hole. Some astronomers suspect that the center of the galaxy listed as M87 is a black hole one billion times more massive than the Sun. Possibly our Milky Way galaxy has a black hole at its center.

What would a trip to a black hole look like? First of all, the term "black hole" is not a very accurate one. A hole is empty space, but those objects we call black holes are fantastically dense balls of matter. They are gravity traps from which nothing seems able to escape.

Imagine that we are traveling through space in our private spaceship and are approaching a black hole dead ahead. We would not be able to see the black hole from our spaceship, but we would see its effects on other things. Instead of blocking a circle of stars from our view, the black hole would seem to push those stars out in all directions so that we would still see them. Instead of being hidden, the image of a star behind the top part of the black hole would be pushed up and be visible above the black hole. The image of a star behind the bottom part of the black hole would be pushed down and be visible below the black hole. If the black hole were moving across the sky, the image of a star right in its path would first be split. Next it would form a rim of light around the black hole. Then as the black hole passed by, the rim of starlight would dissolve once more into a pinpoint of light. A black hole is what astronomers call a gravity lens, a lens that bends the light of objects shining behind it.

GOBLINS

In recent years astronomers have been wondering how small a black hole can be. Maybe they come in many sizes—from the size of a mountain to that of a flea or a germ. These miniature black holes, if they exist, have been named goblins. A goblin sphere the size of a speck of dust would weigh more than a billion tons. Astronomers think of tiny black holes the size of a small lime as containing as much matter as planet Earth. These miniature black holes—again, if they exist—are so massive that they could pass through millions of miles of solid rock before slowing down. Possibly, goblins the size of golf balls or pebbles are made during the explosive crunch that forms a neutron star.

One of the newer ideas about black holes came as a surprise to astronomers when it was announced in 1976. Until then astronomers had thought that nothing could escape from a black hole, not even light, and that black holes gobbled up matter by their powerful gravity, growing more massive as a result. In 1976, in a talk entitled "Black Holes Are White-Hot," the English scientist Stephen Hawking upset the black-hole applecart by turning those ideas inside out.

Hawking said that black holes come in different sizes, including goblins. He also said that very big and very massive black holes were cold, while very small and less massive goblins were white-hot. That meant that goblins gave off light and other forms of energy. That is the idea that upset a lot of astronomers. Tiny goblins with the mass of a large mountain but the size of a germ would be warm objects about room temperature, about 300 kelvins. A goblin with the mass of a small mountain but much smaller than a germ would glow white-hot at perhaps 10,000 kelvins or more. Such objects came to be called white holes.

According to Hawking, black holes change their matter into energy and hurl that energy off into space. So every black hole must be decaying and becoming gradually smaller, moving toward goblinhood. And as it becomes smaller, it becomes hotter. And the hotter it becomes, the brighter it shines and the faster it uses up its matter and gives off energy. Eventually, according to Hawking, *all* of the matter in a black hole must be used up. When that moment comes, when the last piece of the goblin is vanishing, all that is left is a dimming shell of light that keeps dimming until there is nothing left.

The truly massive black holes are at such a low temperature that they use up their matter very slowly and last for billions upon billions of years, according to Hawking's thinking. A goblin with the mass of a mountain and the size of a germ, and that was formed during the Big Bang some 20 billion years ago, vanished fairly recently. Goblins much less massive formed at the same time vanished long ago.

Has anyone ever seen what Hawking has imagined—large and cold black holes giving off energy and as a result slowly changing into tiny and hot white holes that shine in the night? No. These are theories, and today no one knows if they will turn out to be true.

Sometimes astronomers see events in the sky they do not understand. When they do, they invent scientific theories in an attempt to explain those events. An astronomer may think that a certain kind of star or other sky object *should* exist, in order to explain certain things that have been observed, even though such an object has never been seen before. Then other astronomers begin to search the heavens to see if they can find a star or other object like the one that was predicted by theory. That is the way science works, and it is a never-ending search.

THE END: A NEW BEGINNING

Do black holes mark the end of matter in the universe? The answer may be yes. Unless, of course, all of the energy in the universe, along with whatever matter is left, combine as another dense super-atom at some distant future date and explode in another Big Bang. That would start up the universe again. And once again there would be galaxies forming. In them, blue-white superstars, yellow stars like the Sun, red dwarfs, goblins, double stars, nebulae, and other objects that we have described in this book would come to life. Many of those stars, if not most, would have planets. And on some of those planets intelligent life would evolve. Those intelligent beings would look about them at the night sky and wonder what the stars are, how they were formed, and what the future holds.

Astronomy Words
and What They Mean

Apparent brightness   The measure of a celestial object's observed brightness; how bright the object appears to the eye as opposed to its actual brightness, or luminosity. The farther away a light source is from the observer, the less its apparent brightness will be, although its luminosity does not change.

Astronomy   The science dealing with celestial bodies, their distances, luminosities, sizes, motions, relative positions, composition, and structure. The word comes from the Greek and means the "arrangement of the stars."

Atom   The smallest possible piece of an element (see **Element**) that can take part in a chemical reaction. An atom retains all the properties of its element.

Binary star   See **Double star.**

Black dwarf   A star that has passed through the white dwarf stage and is radiating so little energy that it can no longer be observed directly.

Black hole   An incredibly dense and massive star that has burned itself out. Black holes are thought to be so dense that radiation is unable to escape from them; hence, we know of no way of observing them directly.

Blue giant An especially massive, large, and luminous star, such as Rigel (in Orion), which is seen to shine with a bluish white light. The core temperatures and surface temperatures of these short-lived stars are many times higher than those of less massive stars such as the Sun.

Brown dwarf An object with too little mass to become a star. Brown dwarfs are about midway between Jupiter and the smallest true stars in mass. They probably exist throughout the galaxies by the millions. Most are so far away and so dim that detecting them is very difficult.

Cepheid variable A hot white and yellow giant variable star with a period ranging from a few hours to about 50 days. Cepheid variables can be used as cosmic yardsticks to measure distances to galaxies beyond the Milky Way.

Cluster variable A short-period Cepheid variable star with a period of less than a day, so named because it commonly is seen in globular clusters.

Constellation The grouping into an imaginary figure of certain stars on the celestial sphere. The ancients recognized these groups as human and animal figures: for example, Orion, the Hunter; Leo, the Lion; and so on. By international agreement, astronomers recognize a total of 88 constellations.

Density Mass per unit volume, or the amount of matter contained in a given volume of space, and expressed as grams per cubic centimeter. Water, for example, has a density of one gram per cubic centimeter.

Diameter A straight line passing through the center of a circle or sphere and extending from one edge to the opposite edge.

Double star   Two stars held in gravitational association with each other and revolving around a common center of mass. Also called a binary star. Some star systems, such as the one to which Alpha Centauri belongs, have three or more stars held in gravitational association and are known as multiple-star systems.

Dwarf Cepheid   A small Cepheid variable star with a very short period. For example, two that have been studied have periods of 88 minutes and 79 minutes.

Eclipse   The partial or total blocking from view of one celestial object by another passing in front of it. A **stellar eclipse** occurs in a double-star system when one of the two stars revolving about each other passes in front of and blocks out the light of the other star. A **lunar eclipse** occurs when the Moon passes through Earth's shadow. A **partial solar eclipse** occurs when the Moon blocks only part of the Sun from view. In a **total solar eclipse,** the Moon completely covers the Sun's disk. An **annular solar eclipse** occurs when the Moon covers the Sun's disk but, because the moon is at its greatest distance from Earth, it does not appear quite so large as the Sun and so leaves a narrow rim of the Sun visible.

Electron   A negative unit of electricity and part of all atoms. Clouds of electrons surround the nuclei of atoms. The mass of an electron is only a small fraction of the mass of a proton.

Element   A substance made up entirely of the same kinds of atoms. Such a substance cannot be broken down into a simpler substance by chemical means. Examples are gold, oxygen, lead, and chlorine.

Energy   That property of an object enabling it to do work. Stars emit huge amounts of energy in the forms of light, heat, radio waves, X rays, and ultraviolet rays, for example.

Eruptive variable star   A variable star that increases in brightness as a result of exploding mildly or catastrophically.

Flare star   A star that sends out sudden flashes of light and then dims rapidly. Such stars may resume shining normally within a half-hour or so. Proxima Centauri is a flare star.

Flash star   A variable red dwarf star that flashes into brightness and remains bright from a few minutes up to three hours. Several such stars are in the Pleiades star cluster and may be new stars in the process of heating up.

Fusion   See **Nuclear fusion.**

Galaxy   A vast collection of stars, gas, and dust held together gravitationally. **Spiral galaxies,** the brightest of all galaxies, have a dense nucleus with less dense spiral arms. Our galaxy is a spiral galaxy containing a few hundred billion stars. Because the galaxies are oriented every which way in space, we see some edge-on and others from all different angles. **Barred spiral galaxies** have arms that wind outward from the ends of a central bar. Some of them have arms that sweep around so that they nearly touch both ends of the central bar. Barred spirals seem to have unusually large amounts of gas and dust. **Elliptical galaxies** are slightly flattened, sphere-shaped galaxies. While some are very elongated, others form nearly perfect globes. We cannot see any structure in these star systems, nor is there evidence that they contain large clouds of gas and dust. **Irregular galaxies** are so named because they have no regular shape. The nearby galaxies called the Clouds of Magellan are both irregular galaxies.

Globular cluster   A collection of tens or hundreds of thousands of stars forming a globular shape. A halo of about 100 globular clusters forms a sphere around the central part of our galaxy.

Globule   An especially dense concentration of gas and dust that appears to be the first stage of star formation. Globules have been identified in several large nebulae.

Goblin   A small black-hole star from about the size of a mountain to the size of a flea or a germ. Goblins are white holes that radiate energy by using up their mass. See **White hole.**

Gravitation   The force of attraction between any two or more objects in the universe, no matter how large or small. The attraction between any two objects in the universe is directly proportional to their mass and inversely proportional to the square of the distance between them. The greater the mass, the greater the force of attraction; the greater the distance, the less the force of attraction.

Gravity   The gravitational force between Earth, for instance, and any object on its surface or within its gravitational field.

Light-year (L.Y.)   The distance that light travels in one year, at the rate of 299,000 kilometers (186,000 miles) per second, which is about 10 trillion kilometers (6 trillion miles).

Luminosity   The total amount of radiation emitted by an object, or an object's actual brightness. Astronomers usually express luminosity in units called ergs.

Magnitude   Apparent, or visual, magnitude is a convenient way to talk about the relative visual brightness of the stars as we see them in the sky. The higher the magnitude number of a star, the fainter the star appears to us. Some of the nearby brightest stars have a magnitude of 1 and are said to be first magnitude stars. Stars that appear two and a half times dimmer than first magnitude stars have a visual magnitude of 2, and stars appearing two and a half times dimmer than second magnitude stars have a visual magnitude of 3, and so on. The very brightest-appearing sky objects are given negative magnitudes. For example, the Sun has a visual magnitude of −27; the Moon, −10; and a bright comet, about −5. The faintest stars visible to the unaided eye are magnitude 6.

Mass   A given quantity of matter of any kind, or the total quantity of matter contained in an object.

Milky Way   The name of our local galaxy, containing some 300 billion or more stars. Also the name of that hazy band of light seen in the summer and winter sky. A small telescope resolves the band into countless stars.

Mira-type variable   Most pulsating variable stars are of the Mira type, named after the first such star discovered in the constellation Cetus, the Whale. About 4,000 Mira-type variables are listed. The typical period is 300 days.

Nebula   A great cloud of dust and gas within a galaxy. Some nebulae, called **reflection nebulae,** reflect light generated by nearby stars, or by stars embedded within the nebula. Other nebulae are dark and so are called **dark nebulae.** Still others reradiate energy emitted by stars embedded in the nebulae and are called **emission nebulae.** And still others take the form of a great shell of gas cast off by an eruptive, or explosive, star. These are called **planetary nebulae** because they were once mistaken for planets within the Solar System.

Neutron   An electrically neutral particle in the nucleus of all atoms except hydrogen. Neutrons are only slightly more massive than protons. Outside the atom, neutrons have a life of only 20 minutes or so before they decompose into an electron and a proton.

Neutron star   A star made up of neutrons. Because neutrons are without an electrical charge and there is no force of repulsion, they can be packed very closely together. Consequently, neutron stars are extremely dense objects.

Nova   A star that, for some reason not yet fully understood, bursts into brilliance. Within a few days a typical nova may become hundreds of thousands of times brighter than usual, then it becomes somewhat less brilliant, and after a few months or longer the star returns to its pre-nova brightness. Certain planetary nebulae may be the result of nova eruptions.

Nuclear fusion   The union of atomic nuclei and, as a result, the building of the nuclei of more massive atoms. Hydrogen nuclei in the core of the Sun fuse and build up the nuclei of helium atoms. In the process large amounts of energy are emitted, thus accounting for the Sun's energy output.

Nucleus   In astronomy, the central portion of a galaxy or a comet. In chemistry and physics, the central portion of an atom. In biology, the central region of a cell.

Orbit   The path one celestial object traces as it moves around another to which it is attracted by the force of gravitation. Earth and the other planets of the Solar System all have their own orbits around the Sun. The Moon travels in an orbit around Earth, and the Sun travels in an orbit around the nucleus of our galaxy.

Period   The time a variable star takes to complete one cycle of going from bright to dim and back again to bright. The periods of some variables are measured in hours, while the periods of others are measured in weeks or months. Also, the length of time it takes one celestial object to complete one orbit about another.

Planetary nebulae   A nebula such as the Ring Nebula in Lyra, once mistakenly thought to be a planet. The faint greenish color of planetary nebulae gives them the appearance of the planet Uranus.

Planetary system   Any star accompanied by one or more planets. The Solar System is presumably only one of many planetary systems in our and other galaxies.

Planet   A celestial object that shines by reflected light from a star around which it is held gravitationally captive and revolves. There are nine known primary planets in the Solar System.

Pressure   A measurement of force per unit area.

Prominence   A glowing mass of gas that loops and surges from the Sun's surface gases for distances of hundreds of thousands of kilometers. Prominences can best be seen during an eclipse of the Sun or by special instruments such as the coronagraph and the spectrohelioscope.

Proton   A fundamental particle present in the nucleus of all atoms. A proton has a positive charge of electricity equal in strength to the negative charge of an electron, but a proton is 1,840 times more massive than an electron.

Protostar   A newly forming star that has not yet begun to radiate visible energy as a result of fusing hydrogen nuclei into helium nuclei in the star's core region. See **Nuclear fusion.**

Pulsar   A rapidly rotating neutron star that sends out "pulses" of radiation. When the radiation is emitted in the direction of Earth, we receive a pulse. About 150 or so pulsars have been detected; each has its own rate of pulsation.

Recurrent nova   A nova star that explodes more than once but not on any particular schedule. One in Sagitta has been seen to explode at least three times: once in 1913, again in 1946, then again in 1978.

Red dwarf   A star with relatively little mass and a low surface temperature (about 3,000 kelvins), which causes the star to shine with a reddish light.

Red giant   An enormous star that shines with a reddish light because of its relatively low surface temperature (about 3,000 kelvins). It is now thought that most stars go through a red-giant stage after they exhaust their core hydrogen and the core collapses gravitationally. The star then swells up and becomes a red giant.

Revolution   The motion of one celestial body around another. The Moon revolves about Earth; the planets revolve around the Sun.

Rotation   The motion of a body around its axis. The Sun and all of the planets rotate. Earth completes one rotation about every 24 hours.

RR Lyrae variable   A variable star with a period of less than a day. Because all RR Lyrae variables are the same brightness, they can be used as cosmic yardsticks to measure distances within our galaxy.

Shell star   A nova star that blasts away a great gas bubble, or shell, that surrounds the star and appears as a giant smoke ring in space.

Solar System   The Sun, its nine known primary planets accompanied by about 60 or more known satellites, plus many lesser objects, including comets, asteroids, meteoroids, and at least one planetoid.

Solar wind   Streams of charged particles (protons and electrons, for example) blown off by the Sun and sweeping throughout the Solar System.

Star   A hot, glowing globe of gas that emits energy. The Sun is a typical, and our closest, star. Most stars are enormous compared with planets, containing enough matter to make thousands of Earthlike planets. Stars generate energy by the fusion of atomic nuclei in their dense and hot cores. Stars seem to be formed out of clouds of gas and dust, evolve through various stages, and finally end their lives as dark, cold objects called black dwarfs.

Supernova   A giant star whose brightness is tremendously increased by a catastrophic explosion. Supernova stars are many thousands of times brighter than ordinary nova stars. In a single second, a supernova releases as much energy as the Sun does over a period of about 60 years.

Temperature   A measure of how hot or cold a body is, "hotness" meaning the rate of atomic motion, or kinetic energy. The greater the kinetic energy, the "hotter" a substance is said to be.

Variable star   A star that is not uniform in its brightness; one that becomes bright, reaching "maximum," then dims, reaching "minimum." The cycle repeats itself over periods of hours, months, or years.

White dwarf   A very small star that radiates stored energy rather than new energy generated through nuclear fusions. The Sun is destined to become a white dwarf after it goes through the red-giant stage.

White hole   A very small black-hole star that is rapidly changing mass into energy and so shines with a white-hot light.

Index

L

lead, 94
Leonid meteor shower, 5
life-span, stars, 40
light, speed of, 18
light-year, 104
lithium, 39
local hot spots, 75
LP 768-500, 68
luminosity, 38, 104
lunar eclipse, 102
Lupus, the Wolf, 89
Lyra, the Harp, 70, 72, 81, 85

M

M87, 97
magnetism
  Sun, 21
  sunspots, 24
magnitude, 104–105
Mars, 16
mass, 105
  Deneb, 47
  vs. size, 39
matter, 28, 36
meteoroids, 16
meteors, 4
  Leonid shower, 5
Milky Way galaxy, 30, 33, 45–47,
  80, 81, 86, 105
Mira-type variable stars, 78–81, 105
Moon, 16, 102

N

Navajo Canyon, 88
Naval Observatory, U.S., 16–17
nebulae, 33–36, 105

Crab, 87–91
  planetary, 70, 72–73, 105, 107
neutron stars, 91–94, 106
  pulsars, 94–95
neutrons, 20, 105
  in Sun's core, 26–27
NGC 4725 galaxy, 93
NGC 7293 galaxy, 70
nickel, 91
nitrogen, 39
Northern Cross, *see* Cygnus, the
  Swan
Northern Lights, 21, 23
Nova Aquilae, 71
Nova Cygni, 70–71
Nova Herculis, 71–72
novae, 68–72, 78, 84, 106, 108
  see also supernovae
nuclear fusion, 106
nucleus, 106

O

Ophiuchus, the Serpent Bearer, 77,
  89
orbit, 106
Orion, the Hunter, 11, 12, 33, 34–
  36, 37–38, 40, 50, 53, 54–56
oxygen, 39, 91, 92

P

partial solar eclipse, 102
period, 106
  see also variable stars
photosphere, Sun, 23–25
pigmy stars, 65
  see also dwarf stars
Pisces, the Fishes, 12, 65